110
YEARS OF
RUGBY
LEAGUE

110 YEARS OF RUGBY LEAGUE

THE HISTORY. THE HEROES. THE HEART

Team of the Century five-eighth Wally Lewis salutes the SCG faithful at the Centenary Test in 2008.

I've been in love with this game all my life and I'm going to be in love with this game until the day I die. I'm thankful that I've had rugby league grace my life.

I was born into a rugby league family and right from the start, I couldn't get enough of the game.

My dad Jim was a first-grade player at Souths and Wests in Brisbane and my mum June represented Queensland in netball. Dad's crook knee forced him into early retirement but he got into coaching. He couldn't stay away from it.

Even before I was old enough to play, I'd be the mascot for the under-18s team he was coaching at Wynnum Manly.

It was 1963 and I was three years old and I'd go out for the coin toss with the captains. Then I'd get to keep the shilling coin so dad used to joke that I was a professional immediately!

In those days under-8s was as young as you could play and in my first ever game, Dad told me the referee stopped the game and told me to settle down and stop doing everything! I was apparently doing every tackle and he wanted me to settle down. The old man often used to joke that me doing all the tackles didn't last long.

As I got a bit older I'd train during the week and play for my club and my school. I'd watch my brothers play on the weekend, then go to my own game and then to watch the Wynnum teams Dad was coaching.

Before school we'd play footy on the oval and rip into each other until we ended up with a torn shirt or torn pants. At recess we'd have a short game and then at lunchtime you'd have a proper match. It was an obsession and there was never enough time in the day for all the footy I wanted to play.

In those early days the Brisbane Rugby League had our attention and you dreamed about playing first grade for one of the eight clubs. We saw those guys in the BRL as the supermen of the sport.

And it's the same for all the kids today watching guys like Cam Smith and Billy Slater and JT. They idolise them and copy them and hang off their every move.

The passion of the fans is the lifeblood of the sport and I love getting out and talking to them when I go to matches.

I'm proud of these people and I recognise the role they play in the success of the sport.

From the kids holding their parents' hands on the way into the game to the blokes going in for a beer with their mates . . . they are the real heroes.

What makes rugby league so special is that it belongs to people from all walks of life. From doctors and lawyers to sparkies and chippies and their kids. Once they walk through that gate they are all equal. We want to feel like we are part of a team and we are all part of the rugby league circus.

Rugby league is so powerful and so resilient and it provides such a wonderful entertainment factor for the fans who part with their hard-earned cash to come along and watch it.

I've been involved with rugby league my whole life and I was reminded just how much the game has meant to me this year as I worked my way through hundreds of photos to use in a book I'm putting out next year.

It's a look back at my life in footy and I've got 30 boxes of photos and news clippings which centre around family and the things we've done since I fell in love with this great game 55 years ago.

Working on that project at the same time as talking to the author of '110 Years of Rugby League', Martin Lenehan, about my career has brought back so many incredible memories.

It took me back to when I was a young boy listening to the footy on radio 4BH and the caller, George Lovejoy, would sign off at the end of the game the same way every week. He'd say, 'ladies and gentlemen, there we have it', and then he'd give the score, and then say, 'until we meet next time, rugby league football, the greatest game of all'.

You got that right, George.

WALLY LEWIS, Rugby League Immortal

Wally Lewis was made an Immortal in 1999 and selected in the Team of the Century in 2008. He played 34 Tests for Australia, 24 as captain. He played 31 Origins for Queensland, 30 of those as captain, and won a record eight man-of-the-match awards.

Long after the commotion and emotion had died down, the Sharks' 2016 Grand Final hero Andrew Fifita found a moment for reflection – on the very blade of grass where he had stormed over for the match-winning try.

Take a bow, Nathan Hopkins. The NRL photographer captured this magnificent image at Pepper Stadium in April, 2017, on a day when the sun shone but Waqa Blake and his Panthers didn't, beaten 28-2 by the Sharks.

Moses Mbye and his Bulldog buddies battled the Storm and a storm in the opening round of 2017 at Belmore Sports Ground – and were beaten by both. NRL snapper Grant Trouville also braved the elements to capture this cracking shot.

The athleticism of the modern day winger has to be seen to be believed and Dragons veteran Jason Nightingale threw self-preservation out the window as he launched himself at the line in the 2018 season opener against Brisbane.

CONTENTS

INTRODUCTION 14

TRAIL BLAZERS 16

THE LEGENDS 36

THE CLUBS 66

THE KANGAROOS 110

STATE OF ORIGIN 142

THE FANS 168

THE RECORDS 196

INDEX 222

A poignant moment between two giants of the game... Artie Beetson consoles Graeme Langlands after the '75 decider.

For proud and passionate fans of the greatest game of all, rugby league is the gift that keeps giving. From the first time we turned on the radio or TV to follow our team's fortunes, or headed to the ground to soak up the atmosphere, the game has been our lifeblood. A massive hit of adrenalin – an emotional release. A chance to be part of a common cause and stand united as our heroes go into battle. We embrace them all. The flawed and the freakish. The King, Lord Ted and the Prince of Centres. Big Artie and the Little Master. Great players, great men and great memories.

If you close your eyes for just a minute, you can still see that first game as if it were yesterday. Still hear the bone crunching impact as two forwards collide. Still feel the tears on your cheek after your team lost a Grand Final. Still taste the hot dog Wayne Pearce sold you at Leichhardt Oval.

For me, it all started with the white boots. Those bloody white boots worn by the incomparable Graeme Langlands on Grand Final day 1975. The day Chang's Dragons suffered the indignity of a 38-0 drubbing at the hands of Jack Gibson's Roosters.

As if watching my team get smashed wasn't bad enough, the sight of a true legend of the game hobbling around after a painkilling injection numbed his leg, made it even more galling. And just so you didn't miss any of Chang's leading role in the Red V horror show, he was sporting the now infamous white boots, ensuring he stood out for all the wrong reasons.

The image of two future Immortals leaving the field together – Langlands in utter despair and Beetson consoling him – sums up everything that is great about rugby league.

Beetson's team had just gone back-to-back, and posted a record Grand Final margin, but he wasn't about to disrespect a fallen champion by hooting and hollering while Chang limped off.

And so it was, that the first game that stuck in my memory also stuck in my craw. But that didn't stop me coming back in 1976. And every year since then.

That's the power of rugby league. Through the highs and the lows, the winning seasons and the winters of discontent, true footy fans are all-in. No half measures, only full commitment. We embrace the characters. Men like Allan Langer and Billy Smith and Geoff Robinson and Willie Mason and Steve Roach. We marvel at the athleticism of Billy Slater and Sonny Bill Williams. Clive Churchill and Reg Gasnier.

We admire the bravery of . . . every bloody one of them. Whether it was Dave Brown and 'Jersey' Flegg and Arthur Hennessy charging into the unknown in 1908, when there was no limit on tackles and no shortage of flair from Mr Messenger and his mates.

Or the rugged Rabbitohs of the late '60s, led by the peerless Ron Coote and the fearless John Sattler, who mastered the four-tackle era to win three titles in four years.

Or the mercurial Manly men, Ken Irvine, John Mayes and Graham Eadie, taking charge in '72 and '73 when the six-tackle rule had come into vogue and attacking geniuses like Bob Fulton would come into their own.

By 1993, we had the 10-metre rule, and more space meant more room for the stars to shine.

Enter Steve Renouf, Laurie Daley, Cliff Lyons, Andrew Johns and Brad Fittler.

A decade later, golden point extra-time arrived to sort out a winner in drawn matches. Good for some, not so good for others, but never short of drama. As if 80 minutes of tension wasn't enough, tack on 10 more to settle it.

The official line went that drawn games were a letdown for fans and left them with a hollow feeling. As it had countless times down the years, the game moved with the times to maintain its appeal, but still maintained its soul.

It would still be the superstars demanding the ball when the game was on the line. Keeping their heads while all around them are losing theirs. Pulling the strings and working the angles to put their team in a position to prevail.

Enter Johnathan Thurston. Grand Final night 2015. A late Cowboys try had sent the pulsating decider against Brisbane into golden point and the atmosphere at ANZ Stadium was everything we hope for as league fans.

For the 82,758 devotees lucky enough to be there on that balmy October night, this was one for the ages. The pride of Queensland turning Sydney's premier sporting venue into their very own playground for one unforgettable night.

It's history now that Ben Hunt dropped the kick off, Broncos hearts dropped, and Thurston dropped the goal that would change his life. And the lives of every Cowboys fan who'd ridden the rollercoaster since 1995. Bearing the brunt of gibes when three wooden spoons arrived in the mail in their first six years. Experiencing the joy of a trip to the big dance in 2005, only to have Benji give them 'the flick'.

And that's what makes this game so intoxicating and alluring. We live every moment with our heroes. And even when it breaks our heart, we pick up the pieces and front up again the following week.

It's been that way for 110 years.
And it'll be that way for 110 more.

MARTIN LENEHAN, Author

Martin Lenehan has been covering rugby league for 30 years. He joined the game's 'bible', Rugby League Week, in 1995 and was appointed Editor of the magazine in 2003. After nine years at the helm of RLW, he took over as Editor in Chief of Bauer Media's sports titles in 2012. Martin has covered 20 grand finals and more than 60 State of Origin games.

TRAIL BLAZERS

A great game needs big personalities to hoist it up. Rugby league attracted talented, wilful people who saw something bigger, and wouldn't give up until it got there.

110 YEARS OF RUGBY LEAGUE | TRAIL BLAZERS

Rugby league as we know it in 2018 would be unrecognisable to men like Dally Messenger and James Giltinan, but the modern game will forever be linked to those who dug the well.

Known simply as 'The Master', Messenger was both a man for his time and ahead of his time, and his legacy lives on with the medal presented annually to the game's best and fairest player. A brilliant centre with a flair for the unpredictable, Messenger was seen as the key figure when rugby union's best players were looking to break away in 1907 and turn professional.

"Messenger did things that hadn't been thought of and hadn't been done and that's why rules had to be changed," says NRL historian Terry Williams.

"He took it to another level. He didn't study the rules that much but he just had an innate ability to be able to do things in an unorthodox manner. He hadn't grown up besotted with the game – he had done more Aussie Rules and sailing and swimming – but he still changed the way the game was played."

Back when a try was worth just three points, Dally scored four of them and added 10 goals for a personal tally of 32 points for NSW against Queensland. It took 89 years for anyone to equal that mark, with Ryan Girdler scoring three tries and kicking 10 goals for a 32-point haul of his own for the Blues in 2000.

And while Messenger was the prize catch for league in its formative years, Giltinan and Test cricketer Victor Trumper were the men doing the chasing.

Trumper had witnessed first hand the discontent in the rugby union ranks and he and Giltinan saw an opportunity to lure unhappy Wallabies to a new code.

"The problems in rugby had also taken place in cricket so Trumper had seen it all before," Williams continues. "The players resented having an imposed authority that would restrict their rights to make money."

Just as Messenger's legacy lives on with the Dally M Medal, so, too, Giltinan is honoured when the NRL minor premiers are presented with the JJ Giltinan Shield. The Trumper name is front and centre on a grandstand at the Sydney Cricket Ground, which was league's spiritual home until 1988 when the Grand Final was transferred to the Sydney Football Stadium.

And then there's Harry Sunderland, the big daddy of administrators whose name appears on two highly sought after awards in two different hemispheres. In Australia, the Harry Sunderland Medal is awarded to the Kangaroos' best player each year. In England, the man of the match in the Super League Grand Final takes home the Harry Sunderland Trophy.

"Quite simply, Harry made things happen," says Williams. "He may have been regarded as something of a dictator by some people but lots of the really good administrators down through the years have been, for better or worse. The fact his name is on two awards speaks volumes. He was secretary of the Queensland Rugby League for many years and in 1922 he went to Melbourne and got league started down there. He was Kangaroos team manager on the 1929, '33 and '37 tours and later he played a huge role in establishing the game in France."

And so it is that the greatest game of all pays homage to the men who forged a path all those years ago, but for Williams, he'd like to see more pioneers honoured.

Like Edward Larkin, who became the first full-time secretary of the NSWRL in 1909 after Giltinan and Trumper had walked away amid claims of mismanagement.

"Larkin brought a steady hand that allowed rugby league to get some roots and flourish within a few years," Williams recalls.

"Club games in 1909 were only drawing a few hundred people but the Maori tour that came to Australia that year attracted crowds of 20,000, and that meant money.

"That was when a wave of Wallabies decided to switch over, including the captain Chris McKivat and vice-captain Paddy McCue. Once those two guys had gone across to league there was no going back, and others followed.

"They were aware of the opportunities league presented and they were aware of their value. The Wallabies had generated more money than the Kangaroos, but the players saw none of it and had to pay their own way to tour.

"By the end of 1909 players could see that rugby league had legs and wasn't about to fall over.

"Once the quality players were going over to league, then the ones who were still in union started thinking, 'that's the cool place to be' and they went across.

"Under Larkin, the game spread to the country and into schools and he was even looking at the possibility of playing night football. He was a man ahead of his time.

"By 1914 he had been elected to parliament as the first Labor member on Sydney's North Shore and he wanted to get out of league and concentrate on doing a job for greater society. But the British Lions were here and the controversy around the Rorke's Drift Test blew up and they needed him to control that.

"He was trying to have a parliamentary career as well and had two kids under the age of four when he enlisted. Tragically, he went off and was killed on the first Anzac Day at Gallipoli."

Taken way too soon at just 34, Larkin had made an indelible mark off the field, just as Messenger had done on it.

Sadly, Messenger's tale would also have a sad epitaph as he passed away in Gunnedah in 1959, far from the spotlight and with little money to his name. After retiring from his job as a carpenter, he spent the last 25 years of his life touring country areas of NSW spreading the league gospel to kids.

"In many ways, Dally had a troubled life away from football," Williams says. "And he wasn't immune from tragedy."

The essence of our game is captured in the 1963 Gladiators' image of St George's Norm Provan and his Magpies counterpart Arthur Summons. The Sun-Herald's John O'Gready took the photo and Norm and Arthur took their place in history.

Dally Messenger was lauded as a 'freak' by another giant of league's earliest days, Frank Burge.

110 YEARS OF RUGBY LEAGUE | TRAIL BLAZERS

The Blues' Ryan Girdler takes the spoils after equalling Dally Messenger's record of 32 points in an interstate match in Origin Three, 2000 in Sydney.

Captained by Chris McKivat, the 1911-12 Kangaroos squad also contained four Kiwis, by way of trying to help promote the game in New Zealand.

Taking Dally home: Storm champion Cameron Smith picked up his second Dally M Medal in 2017. Testament to his longevity, it came 11 years after his first.

His master's voice: the great Dally Messenger retreated from the spotlight in his later years and gave back to the game by passing his knowledge on to eager youngsters.

Norm Provan made the Sydney Cricket Ground his own during the '50s and '60s, winning a phenomenal 10 premierships with St George, including four as captain-coach.

Harry Sunderland (centre) was a man who made things happen.

110 YEARS OF RUGBY LEAGUE | TRAIL BLAZERS

John O'Gready had every right to be proud of the magical muddy moment he'd captured in 1963, and in 2013 the NRL Premiership Trophy was renamed the Provan Summons Trophy in a fitting tribute to two great warriors and the man who immortalised them.

Harold Horder was the benchmark for wingers, scoring an astonishing 239 tries in 194 senior matches across a 15-year career. His pairing with Cec Blinkhorn at North Sydney in 1921, and later that year on the Kangaroo tour, is regarded as one Australia's finest ever wing combinations.

C M'KIVAT
(Glebe).

P. M'CUE
(Newtown).

110 YEARS OF RUGBY LEAGUE | TRAIL BLAZERS

C. RUSSELL
(Newtown).

Wallaby captain Chris McKivat was a priority signing for rugby league and he came across to the fledgling code for £200. His vice-captain Paddy McCue had been part of McKivat's Gold Medal-winning Wallabies at the 1908 Olympics before coming across in 1909. Charles Russell also won Gold in London and later became a dual international. He was captain-coach of Newtown's 1910 premiership side.

Next stop, rugby league: the First Wallabies of 1908 included future league luminaries Paddy McCue (third row, fifth from left), Peter Burge (third row, fourth from left), Chris McKivat (second row, second from left), Arthur McCabe (back row, fourth from left) and Charles Russell (second row, far right).

110 YEARS OF RUGBY LEAGUE | TRAIL BLAZERS

Albert 'Son' Burge and his brothers Peter, Frank and Laidley all played for Glebe (above) while the Burgess boys Tom, George, Luke and Sam made history in 2013 when they became the first set of four brothers to play in the same team since the Normans – Ray, Rex, Roy and Bernie – at Annandale in 1910.

Influential administrator Edward Larkin (above) and South Sydney's two-time premiership-winning coach Arthur Hennessy (right) were key figures in league's formative years.

34

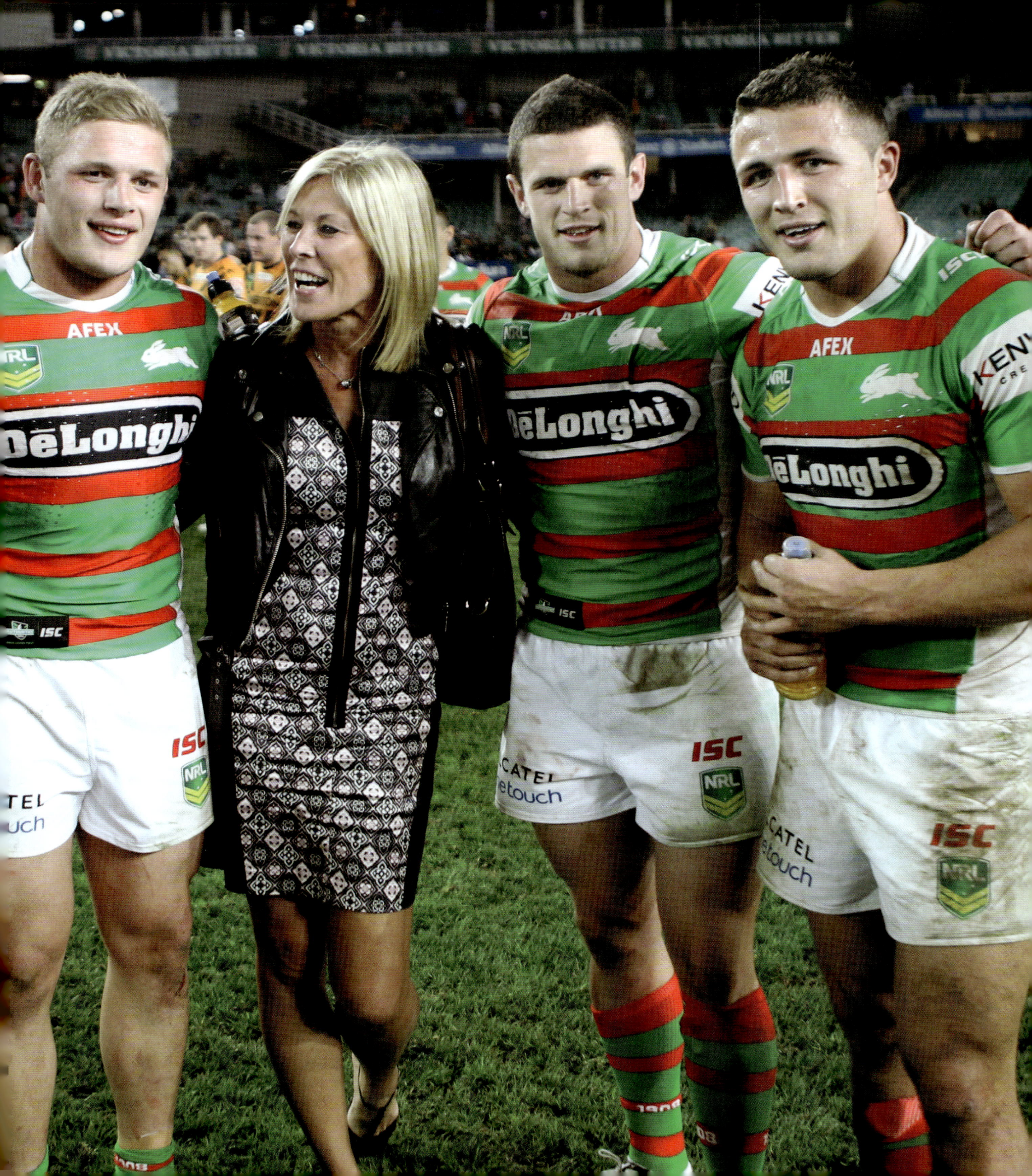
AFEX
DeLonghi
ISC
NRL

THE LEGENDS

From Immortals to Invincibles, Brown to Beetson, King Wally to the Prince of Centres, meet the men who did things mere mortals can only dream of. The men who carry the tag 'legend' as if it was invented just for them.

Of all the qualities which set true champions apart, the ability to overcome physical and mental adversity, to rise from the canvas when staying down would be the easiest option, is perhaps the most admirable.

Feats of heroism and bravery are dotted through the pages of rugby league's history, each one reminding us why we love the game and revere the people who play it.

Take Immortal Clive Churchill, who broke his arm in the early stages of a game against Manly in 1955 but saw out the game thanks to a painkiller and a makeshift splint cobbled together using the cardboard cover of an exercise book. One of his last acts in that game was to calmly slot a conversion from the sideline in the dying minutes to win it for Souths.

Some 62 years later, another goalkicker with nerves of steel, one Johnathan Thurston, defied his own busted wing to ice a memorable Queensland victory in Game Two of the 2017 State of Origin series at ANZ Stadium.

A virtual passenger the entire second half as he nursed a shoulder injury that would require a reconstruction just days later, the Maroons maestro put the pain aside to pilot the conversion of Dane Gagai's try through the sticks for a typically courageous Queensland win, 18-16.

And how about Dave Brown, the man dubbed the 'Bradman of league', whose resilience was severely tested long before he even donned the famous Roosters jersey and began setting tryscoring and pointscoring records which will never be eclipsed.

Born in 1913, Brown joined Easts while still a schoolboy at Waverley College, having already overcome the loss of the top of his right thumb in a lawnmowing accident as a young boy, and an horrific arm injury at school in which he dislocated his elbow and damaged ligaments and nerves.

He would later lose the use of two fingers on his right hand and lose all his hair due to illness but, despite all this, the man with the silky skills and laser boot would amass 93 tries and 194 goals in 94 matches for Easts, steering the Bondi boys to a trifecta of titles from 1935-37.

On one golden May day at the Sydney Sports Ground in 1935, Brown bagged 45 points as Easts did a number on Canterbury to the tune of 87-7. His haul included five tries, part of an astonishing 38 tries for the season.

The record for most points in a match and most tries in a season have been Brown's for 83 years and will surely be his for another 83.

None of this would have been possible, of course, had Brown wallowed in self-pity and not followed his dream.

Like all the people we hail as legends of our game, Brown had a presence that set him apart from his peers.

Whether it's diminutive dynamos like Churchill and Allan Langer using their dancing feet to run rings around the big men, or the incomparable Artie Beetson revolutionising front-row play despite battling weight issues, the greats are rarely ruffled but regularly regal.

"I was lucky enough to share my time with some of the greatest players that ever played the game, but there was only one person who stopped everyone in the room as soon as he entered and that was Arthur," says Queensland Origin legend Chris Close.

"I've never seen anyone capture that space like Arthur did. His charisma and ability to turn heads was just amazing."

At 21, Close was part of a posse of brash young Maroons who entered the Lang Park cauldron under Beetson's guidance in the first ever State of Origin match on July 8, 1980.

Wally Lewis and Mal Meninga, who would go on to play a staggering 63 Origins between them, were just 20 at the time.

"Arthur had that aura, that presence, that made him such an enjoyable person to be around," recalls Lewis.

"You'd hear a hundred stories, like eating a meat pie before a Test match, and obviously there was a fair bit of urban myth attached to most of the stories, but they helped create a legend that will never die.

"A lot of people never got to see big Artie play but you listen to the stories and you'd think they were best mates with him.

"It didn't just create a legend for the person but it was a massive benefit for rugby league in general that blokes like Artie and Graeme Langlands and Bob Fulton were creating this effect, because people wanted to be part of it.

"They created a wonderful aura and the game was the beneficiary."

And on April 17, 2008 in Sydney, the game repaid that debt to its legends when they marked rugby league's centenary by naming the Team of the Century.

One by one they were called to the stage and presented with a magnificent Team of the Century blazer, a moment Lewis holds among the most treasured of his career.

Flanked by fellow Immortals Fulton, Langlands, John Raper, Andrew Johns and Reg Gasnier, as well as Meninga, Norm Provan, Ron Coote and Noel Kelly, Lewis could scarcely believe the company he was in.

"That was a moment in my life I'll never forget. Having a photo up on stage and looking sideways at the blokes I was with, I thought 'how good does this feel'. I still get goose bumps on my arms just thinking about that night.

"I just kept looking around and thinking 'these are the blokes that created the history of rugby league'."

And for that, we thank them all.

John Raper was still a teenager when he debuted for Newtown in 1957. The man they call 'Chook' would play 35 games for the Jets before moving to St George and carving out a career as one of the all-time greats.

The Prince of Centres, Reg Gasnier, was an eloquent speaker and a man of true class.

110 YEARS OF RUGBY LEAGUE | **THE LEGENDS**

The game's original Immortals – Clive Churchill, Bob Fulton, John Raper and Reg Gasnier – posed for this iconic photo at the Sydney Cricket Ground in 1981.

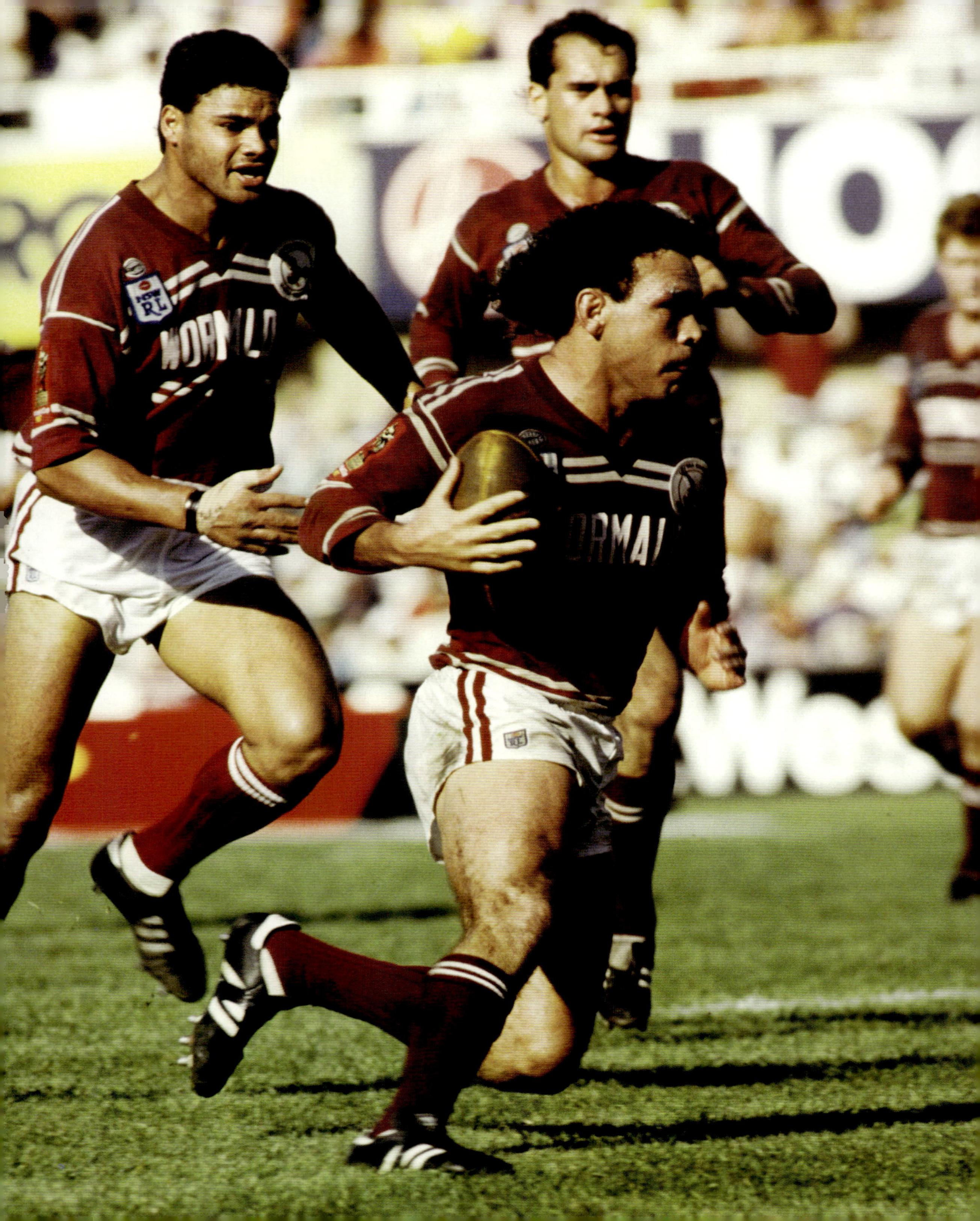

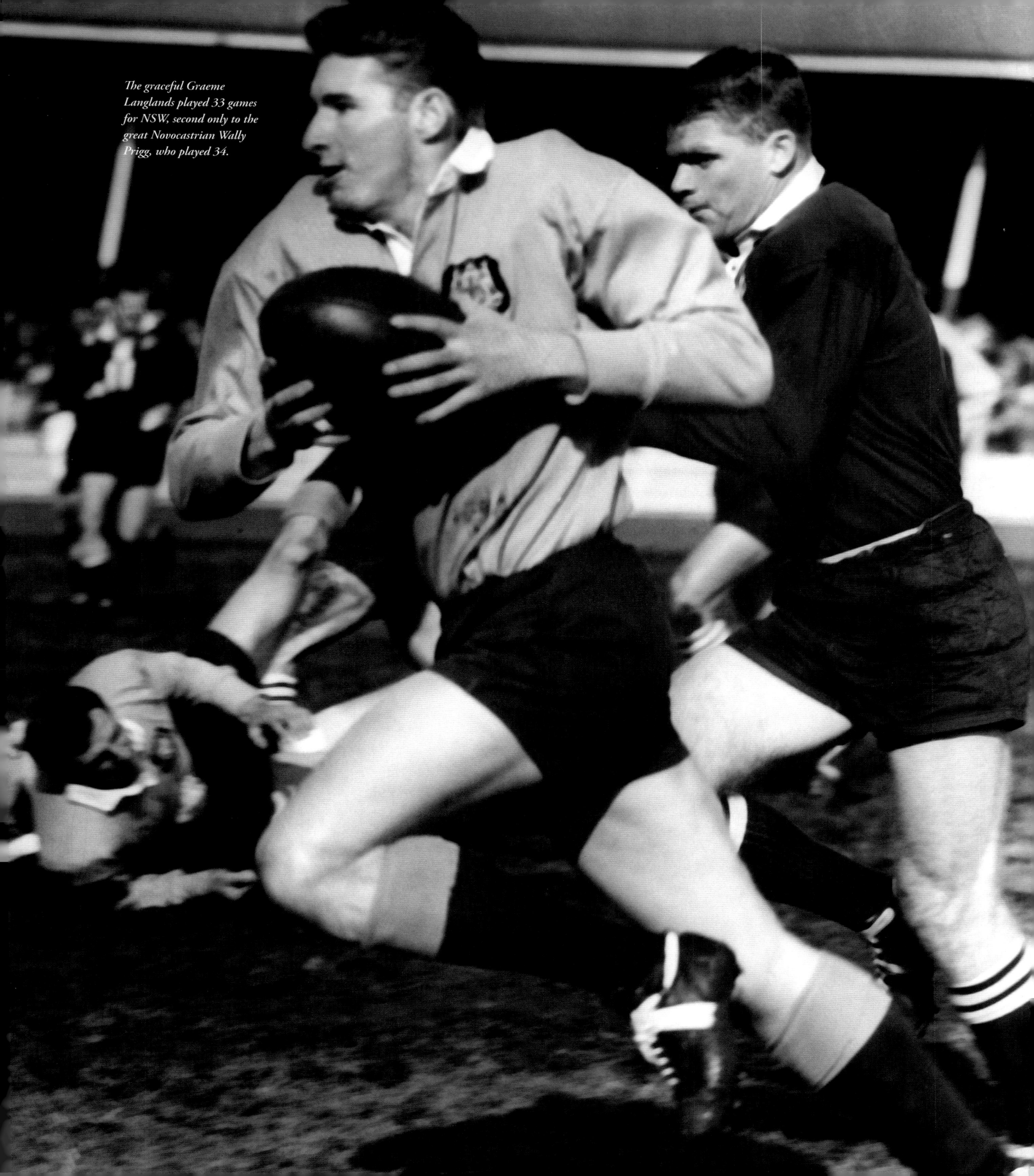

The graceful Graeme Langlands played 33 games for NSW, second only to the great Novocastrian Wally Prigg, who played 34.

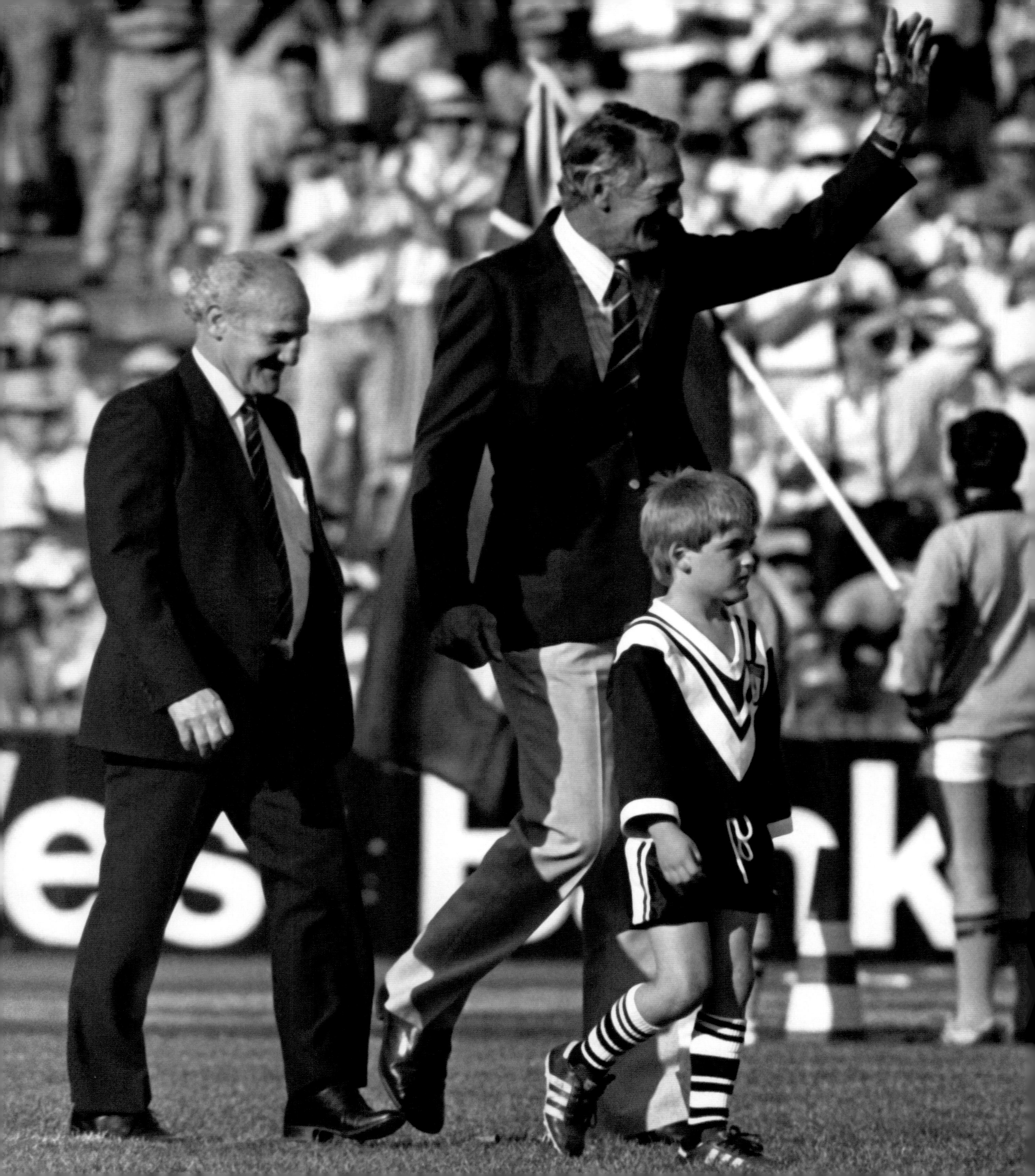

110 YEARS OF RUGBY LEAGUE | THE LEGENDS

Ray 'Rabbits' Warren, began his career at radio station 2LF in Young and spent time at Channel Ten before moving to Channel Nine and becoming the voice of rugby league. In 2014, he was awarded an OAM.

Arthur Summons and Norm Provan received a heroes' welcome every time they stepped out among the adoring league public.

45

Rampaging Rabbitoh Bob McCarthy farewells his family before embarking on the Kangaroos' successful 1970 World Cup tour. A member of the South Sydney Dream Team, McCarthy is widely regarded as one of the finest second-rowers ever to lace a boot.

110 YEARS OF RUGBY LEAGUE | **THE LEGENDS**

In the presence of greatness: Bob McCarthy and Denis Pittard share a joke with Brazilian soccer superstar Pele.

110 YEARS OF RUGBY LEAGUE | THE LEGENDS

One of the true legends of the women's game in Australia, Ruan Sims was the first female to sign a player's contract in the NRL, and the 36-year-old has led her state and country to victories on the biggest stages.

Shouldering the burden: Johnathan Thurston added another chapter to his Boy's Own tale when he defied excruciating pain to land a match-winning conversion for Queensland in Origin Two 2017. Just days later, Thurston was undergoing a shoulder reconstruction. His heroics revived memories of the great Clive Churchill soldiering on with a broken arm and landing a sideline conversion to seal a crucial win for Souths over Manly in 1955.

Balmain, NSW and Kangaroos champion Wayne Pearce trained like a demon and filled his tank with healthy food before leaving nothing in that tank every time he played.

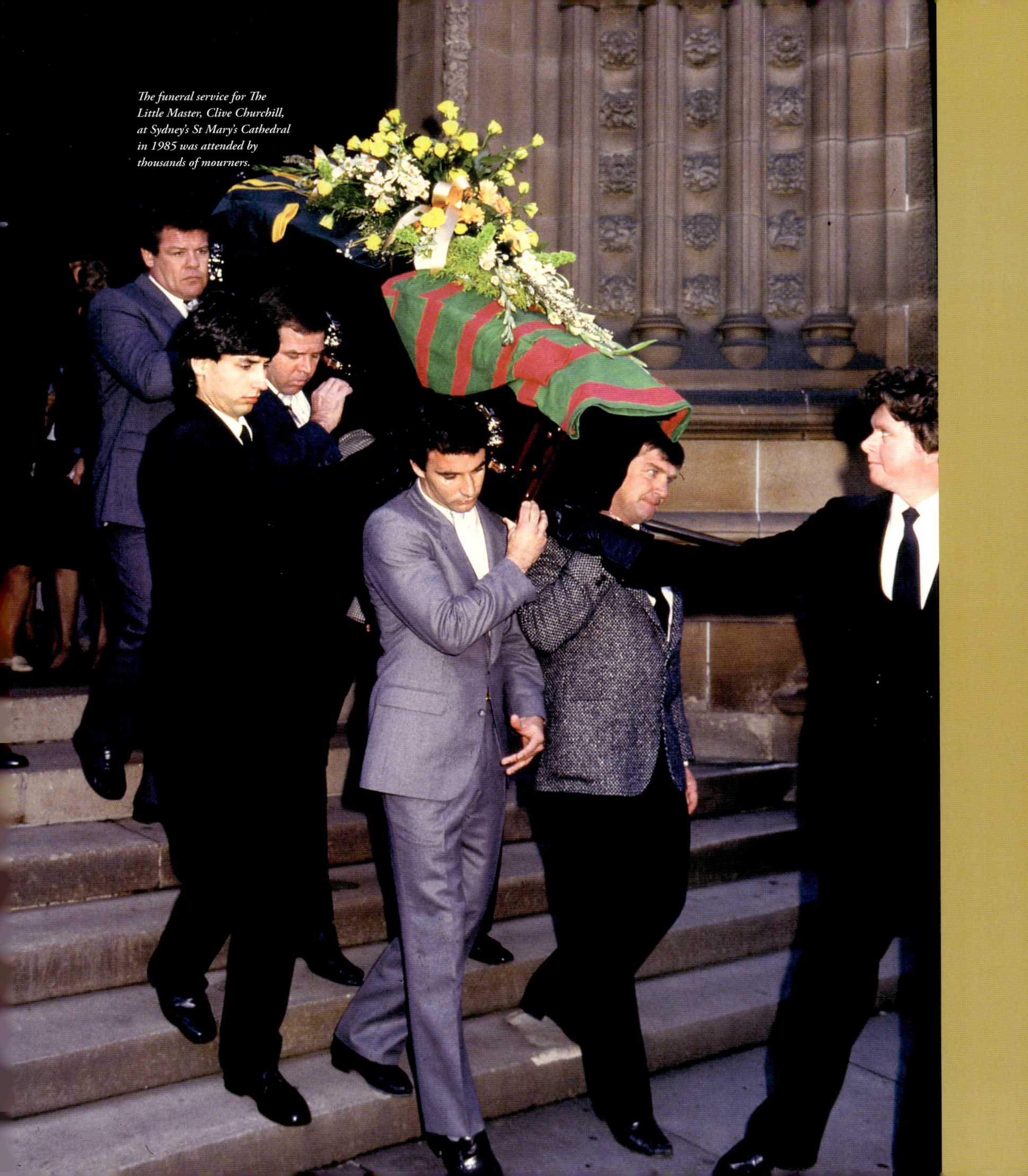

The funeral service for The Little Master, Clive Churchill, at Sydney's St Mary's Cathedral in 1985 was attended by thousands of mourners.

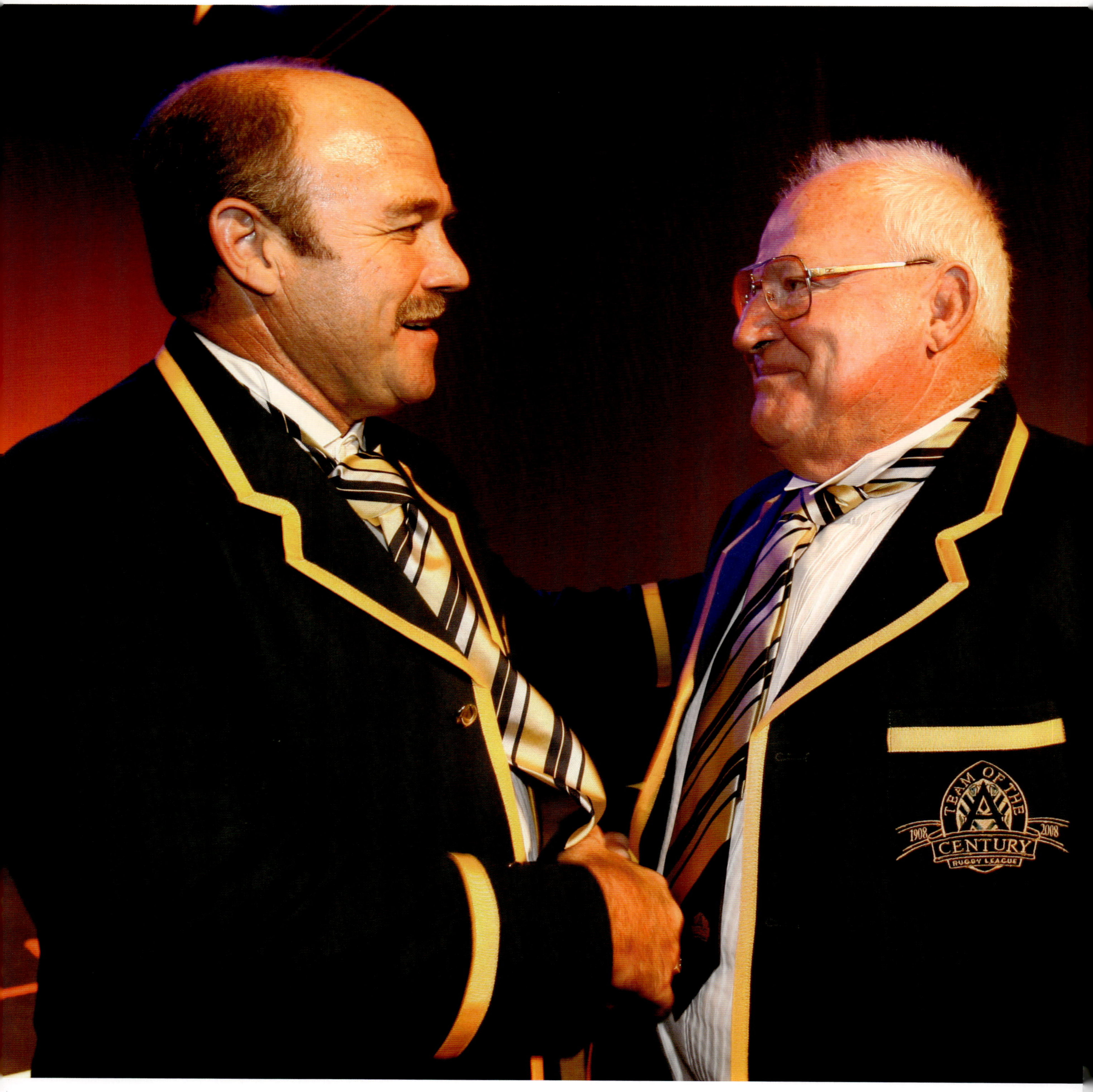
TEAM OF THE
1908
2008
CENTURY
RUGBY LEAGUE

110 YEARS OF RUGBY LEAGUE | **THE LEGENDS**

Night of nights: In 2008 the game honoured its champions by naming a Team of the Century, which included such luminaries as Wally Lewis and Noel Kelly (left). Family members of deceased players were on hand to represent their loved ones and join in the 'team' photo. The Team of the Century is Clive Churchill, Brian Bevan, Reg Gasnier, Mal Meninga, Ken Irvine, Wally Lewis, Andrew Johns, Arthur Beetson, Noel Kelly, Duncan Hall, Norm Provan, Ron Coote, John Raper. Int: Graeme Langlands, Dally Messenger, Bob Fulton, Frank Burge.

Fifty years of pain. Fifty years of frustration. Fifty years of being the butt of jokes. All washed away on Grand Final night 2016 when the Sharks broke their premiership drought – and didn't these two blokes love it! Andrew Ettingshausen was the heart and soul of the club from 1983 to 2000, playing 328 games and leading the club to the 1997 Super League decider. And Paul Gallen. Captain Courageous. The only other Shark to play 300 games and the man who would finally bring the Holy Grail to the Shire. And to put the icing on the cake for the man who captured this historic embrace, NRL Lead Photographer Grant Trouville, it became the first sports photo to win the Walkley Award for photograph of the year. Trouville recalls charging onto the field at full-time and making Gallen the focus of his attention. As the Sharks' spiritual leader collapsed to the turf, exhausted and elated, Trouville snapped away. He thought those shots of Gallen crying would be the pick of the night, but then Gallen was on the move and Trouville sensed something special was about to unfold. "I saw Gal lift his hands up and move fairly quickly towards someone and I realised it was ET, and just as they embraced I was in the perfect spot as they both turned towards me for a split second," Trouville says. "There were a few other snappers but I got the iconic moment. I made the photo black and white to submit to the Walkleys and it really popped." Just like the champagne corks in the Shire.

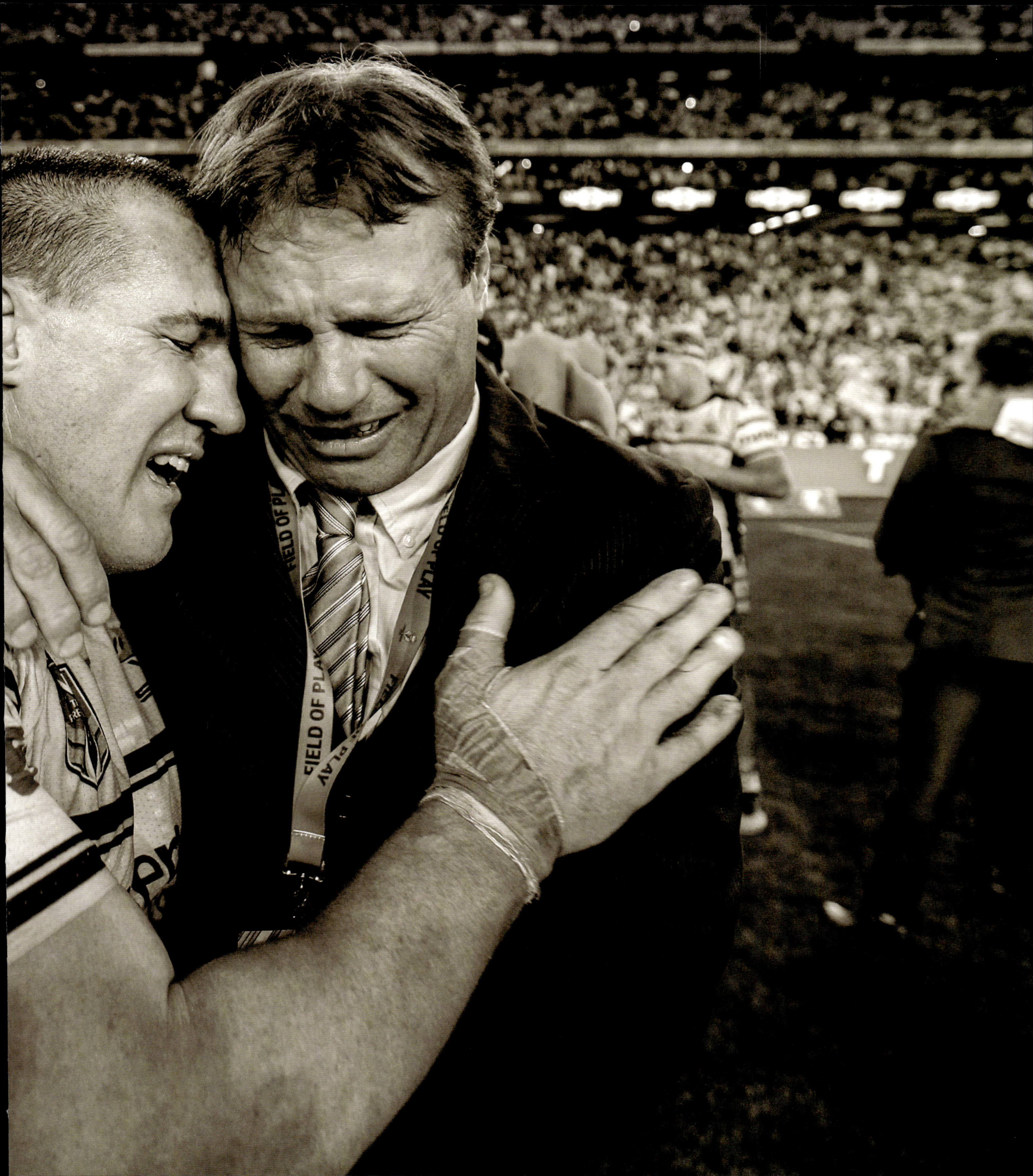
FIELD OF PLAY
FIELD OF PLAY

110 YEARS OF RUGBY LEAGUE | **THE LEGENDS**

All The King's men: Wally Lewis wound down his magnificent career with a stint at the Gold Coast Seagulls in the early '90s. It may not have produced many wins but it gave Lewis the chance to farewell the likes of Brett Kenny (above) and Mal Meninga (right) with one last showdown.

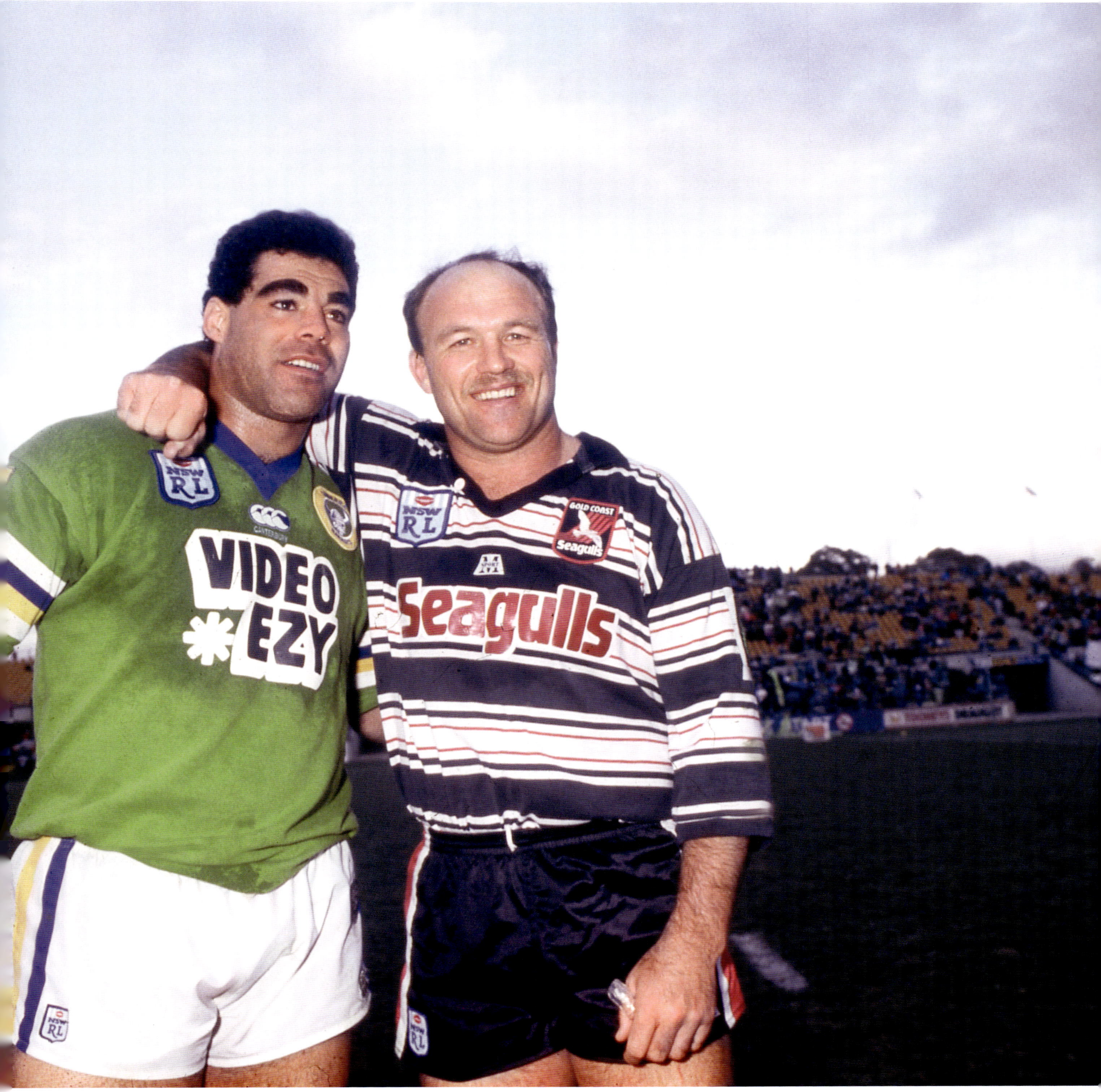
NSW RL
VIDEO
EZY
NSW RL
GOLD COAST
Seagulls
Seagulls

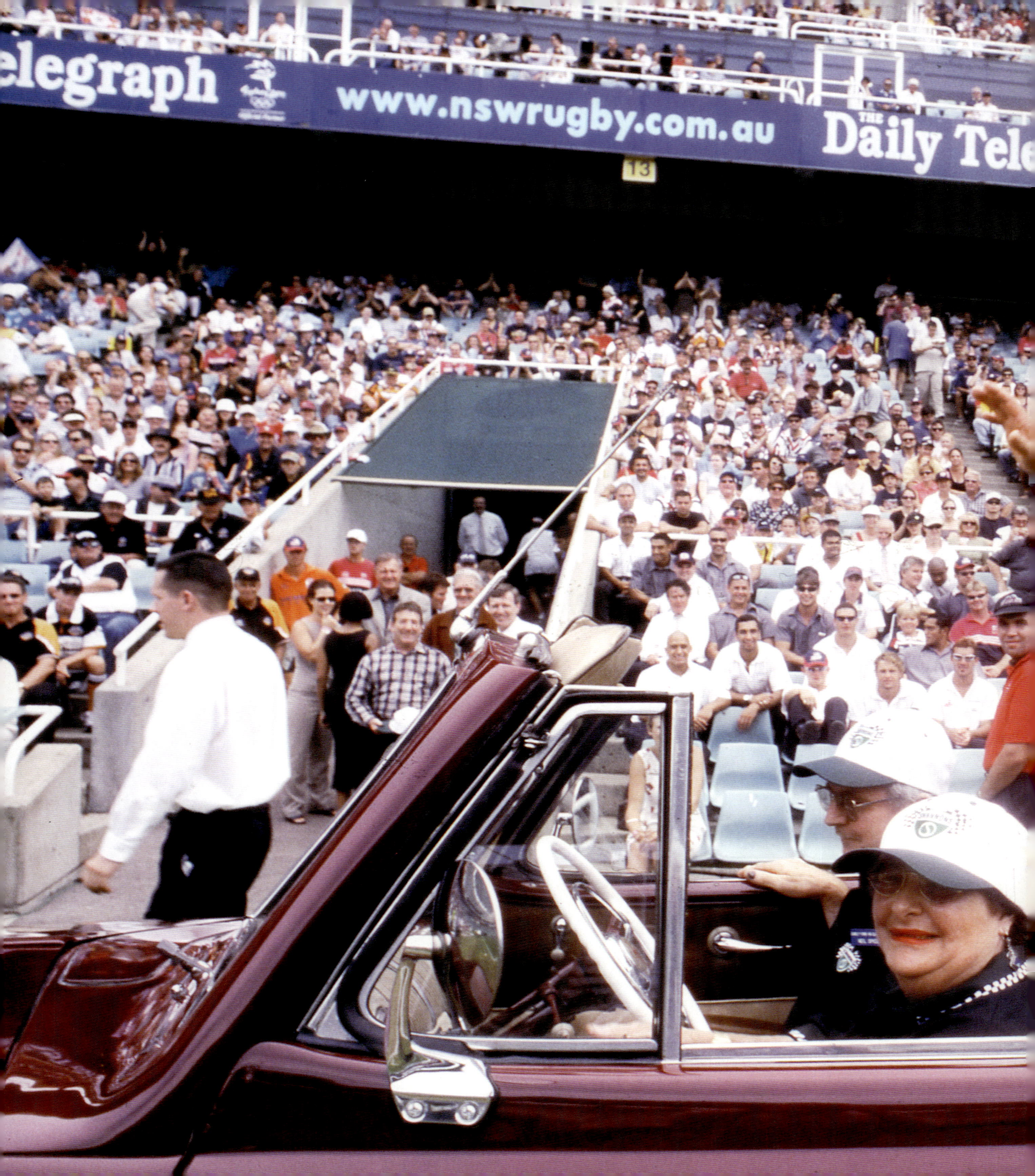
elegraph
www.nswrugby.com.au
THE Daily Tele
13

Loved and revered wherever he went, Arthur Beetson was the first Indigenous Australian to captain Australia in any major sport. He became an Immortal in 2003 and we sadly lost him to a heart attack in 2012.

A piece of Benji Marshall brilliance lit up Telstra Stadium on October 2, 2005 as the Wests Tigers wizard laid on a try for a rampant Pat Richards with an audacious flick pass.

110 YEARS OF RUGBY LEAGUE | **THE LEGENDS**

Fourteen years after she thrilled the nation by winning Olympic Gold at Stadium Australia, Cathy Freeman was back at her field of dreams to see another Indigenous role model Greg Inglis realise his dream by helping South Sydney to a premiership.

61

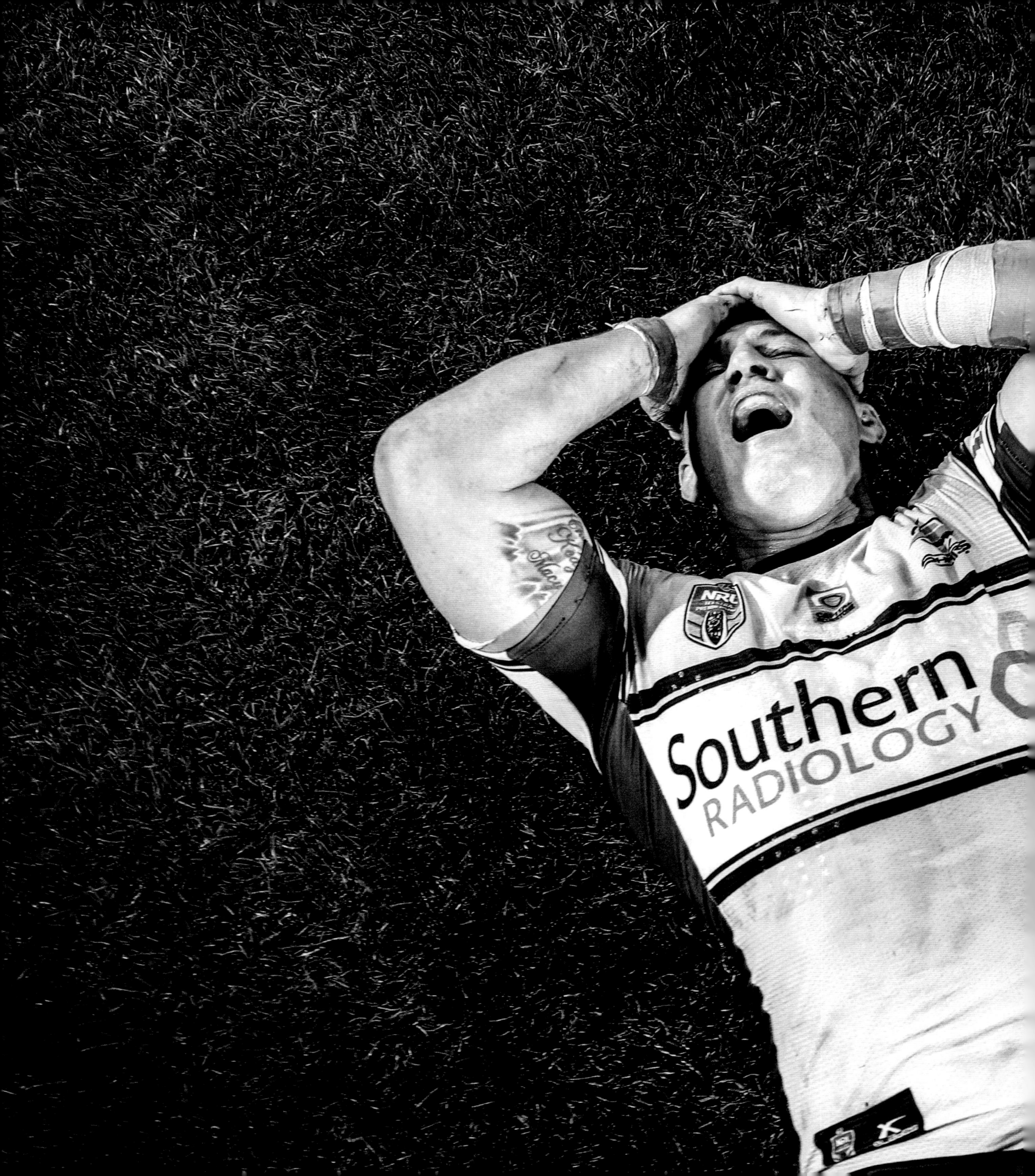
Southern
RADIOLOGY

In the moments immediately following the Sharks' heart-stopping 2016 grand final triumph, skipper Paul Gallen sunk to the turf to reflect on all he had given the club through 279 games and how it had repaid him with the ultimate gift.

110 YEARS OF RUGBY LEAGUE | **THE LEGENDS**

Two of Queensland's favourite sporting sons, former Test wicket-keeper Ian Healy and Broncos great Allan Langer, share a refreshment after taking part in a charity cricket match.

Colourful whistle blower Greg 'Hollywood' Hartley loved to be in the thick of the action. Here he passes on some scrummaging tips to Canterbury rake George Peponis. At the height of his game, Hartley took charge of five grand finals in the late '70s and early '80s.

THE CLUBS

You love them when they're winning ... and love them much less when they aren't. But a true fan has their club's crest written on their heart.

110 YEARS OF RUGBY LEAGUE | THE CLUBS

From the foundation clubs to the clubs that rocked the game's foundations during the Super League War. From South Sydney's long and distinguished history to the short-lived existence of the Hunter Mariners. From the incomparable Dragons' 11-straight premierships, to the North Sydney Bears, stuck on two premierships and seemingly destined never to get a shot at a third.

The history, the heroes, the hardships: every rugby league club has a unique tale to tell, whether it has played out over 110 seasons or flamed out in the space of three.

When the trail was being blazed in 1908, the competition boasted nine clubs: Cumberland, Glebe, Newcastle, Newtown, North Sydney, South Sydney, Balmain, Western Suburbs and Eastern Suburbs.

By 1910, Cumberland and Newcastle were gone, Annandale had joined the fray and the Rabbitohs already had two titles, thanks to captain Arthur Conlin and coach Arthur Hennessy.

The Bunnies' success was built around Hennessy's belief that the running game was king. "When he first got his hands on a rulebook, Hennessy proclaimed 'this is a game for race horses'," says NRL historian Terry Williams. "He was one of the guys who founded Souths and it was under his coaching that the Bunnies' philosophy of 'don't kick the ball' was born."

A golden era soon followed for Easts, who won three titles on the trot from 1911-13, with the game's first superstar Dally Messenger doing the business as captain and coach.

Balmain would then go back-to-back-to-back from 1915-17, with Bill Kelly as captain-coach for the first of the premierships and champion halfback Arthur 'Pony' Halloway at the helm for the next two.

The captain-coach caper was well and truly in vogue during the game's formative years. Others to taste premiership glory in the dual role were Alf Blair at Souths in 1927, and Frank McMillan at Wests in 1934.

Incredibly, come the '50s and '60s, no less than 14 of the 20 premierships were taken out by clubs with a captain-coach: Jack Rayner at Souths in 1950, '51, '53, '54 and '55; Ken Kearney at St George in 1957, '58, '59 and '60; Norm 'Sticks' Provan at St George in 1962, '63, '64 and '65; and Ian Walsh leading the Red V to their 11th title on the trot in 1966.

Kearney was renowned for making his teams train longer and harder and with sharper focus than any coach of the era. The man they called 'Killer' introduced the straight-line defence and few teams could penetrate the red brick wall his men put up.

A testament to the Dragons' aggressive defence is the fact that in the four Grand Finals they won with Kearney as captain-coach, they conceded a total of just 24 points, including holding Manly scoreless in 1959.

Remarkably, the highest Grand Final score by any opponent during the Red V's 11-year reign was 12 by Balmain, in 1956. None of the others even reached double figures!

In the five decades since St George's dominance ended, the most consecutive titles won by any club has been Parramatta's three-peat in 1981-83.

For a club that had collected nine wooden spoons in its first 15 seasons, including six on the trot between 1956-61, their maiden premiership was a moment to treasure.

The signs of a rebirth were there when Terry Fearnley guided the Eels to successive Grand Finals in 1976-77, and a Preliminary Final in 1979 – but only a title would fully satisfy the Blue and Gold Army.

With supercoach Jack Gibson calling the shots, they broke their 34-year drought on September 27, 1981 when a Brett Kenny double helped sink Tommy Raudonikis' Jets. The sublimely gifted Kenny would follow that up with two tries in each of the next two deciders, breaking Manly's hearts in both '82 and '83.

"Jack had a lot of presence about him and he didn't have to say too much to motivate us. But what he did say had substance," says Eels great Peter Wynn. "And our captain Steve Edge was a cool character and a great leader in so many ways.

"He was just a winner. He'd already won two Grand Finals at St George and then he led us to three in a row.

"I can still picture all those people back at the Leagues Club and at our home ground Cumberland Oval in '81. Some time after midnight they burned the grandstand down at Cumberland! They had high expectations that a new stadium was going to be built on the site so they took it upon themselves to start the demolition."

The pure elation of a club's maiden title is something Raiders legend Laurie Daley also relates to, having savoured Grand Final glory in 1989 as a 19-year-old.

"People said Canberra was a city without soul but the Raiders gave them a soul," Daley offers. "We'd been in the comp since '82 and we were the first team from outside Sydney to win it.

"No-one had heard a lot about Glenn Lazarus and Brad Clyde and Ricky Stuart, but they certainly made their marks in '89.

"We developed a siege mentality and we were able to fly under the radar because we weren't under as much scrutiny as other teams. Lots of our players weren't from the Canberra area so they bonded together even tighter and that's where one-team towns can thrive and excel. Your families get to know each other, you support each other and you become a united group.

"We had great senior players like Mal Meninga leading the way and if the senior guys are the ones driving the culture, then the others are too scared to put a foot out of order because they'll come down on you like a tonne of bricks."

Sounds an awful lot like the blueprint being used by modern-day masters the Melbourne Storm.

Happy 21st: Jubilant Bunnies fans lap up the 2014 grand final success with two of their heroes, John Sutton and Greg Inglis. The premiership was the 21st in the foundation club's proud history.

That tackle! Panther Scott Sattler cuts down runaway Rooster Todd Byrne with one of the most famous tackles in Grand Final history. The scores were tied 6-all at the time but Sattler's chase inspired Penrith, who went on to win 18-6.

110 YEARS OF RUGBY LEAGUE | THE CLUBS

Nice one, Dad: Sharks captain Paul Gallen shares a special moment with son Kody after the 2016 Grand Final.

110 YEARS OF RUGBY LEAGUE | THE CLUBS

Sam Burgess channelled the spirit of John Sattler 44 years earlier when he played 79 minutes with a fractured cheekbone to lead Souths to glory in 2014. And team owner Russell Crowe loved it! This shot by the NRL's Robb Cox had 1.4 million views on Facebook and Instagram, launching a new era for footy on social media.

The Everywhere Man: Mr Mercurial, Phil Blake, had stints at Manly, Souths, Norths, Canberra, St George and Auckland between 1982 and '97.

THE CLUBS

THEN . . .

Adelaide 1997-98

Annandale 1910-1920

Cumberland 1908

Glebe 1908-1929

Gold Coast 1988-1998

Hunter Mariners 1997

Newcastle 1908-1909

Newtown 1908-1983

Northern Eagles 2000-2002

North Sydney 1908-1999

South Queensland 1995-1997

Western Reds 1995-1997

University 1920-1937

St George 1921-1998

Illawarra 1982-1998

Balmain 1908-1999

Wests 1908-1999

AND NOW . . .

South Sydney 1908 – 2018

Sydney Roosters 1908-2018

Brisbane 1988-2018

Canberra 1982-2018

Canterbury 1935-2018

Cronulla 1967-2018

Gold Coast Titans 2007-2018

Manly 1947-2018

Melbourne 1998-2018

Newcastle Knights 1988-2018

North Queensland 1995-2018

Parramatta 1947-2018

Penrith 1967-2018

St George Illawarra 1999-2018

Warriors 1995-2018

Wests Tigers 2000-2018

73

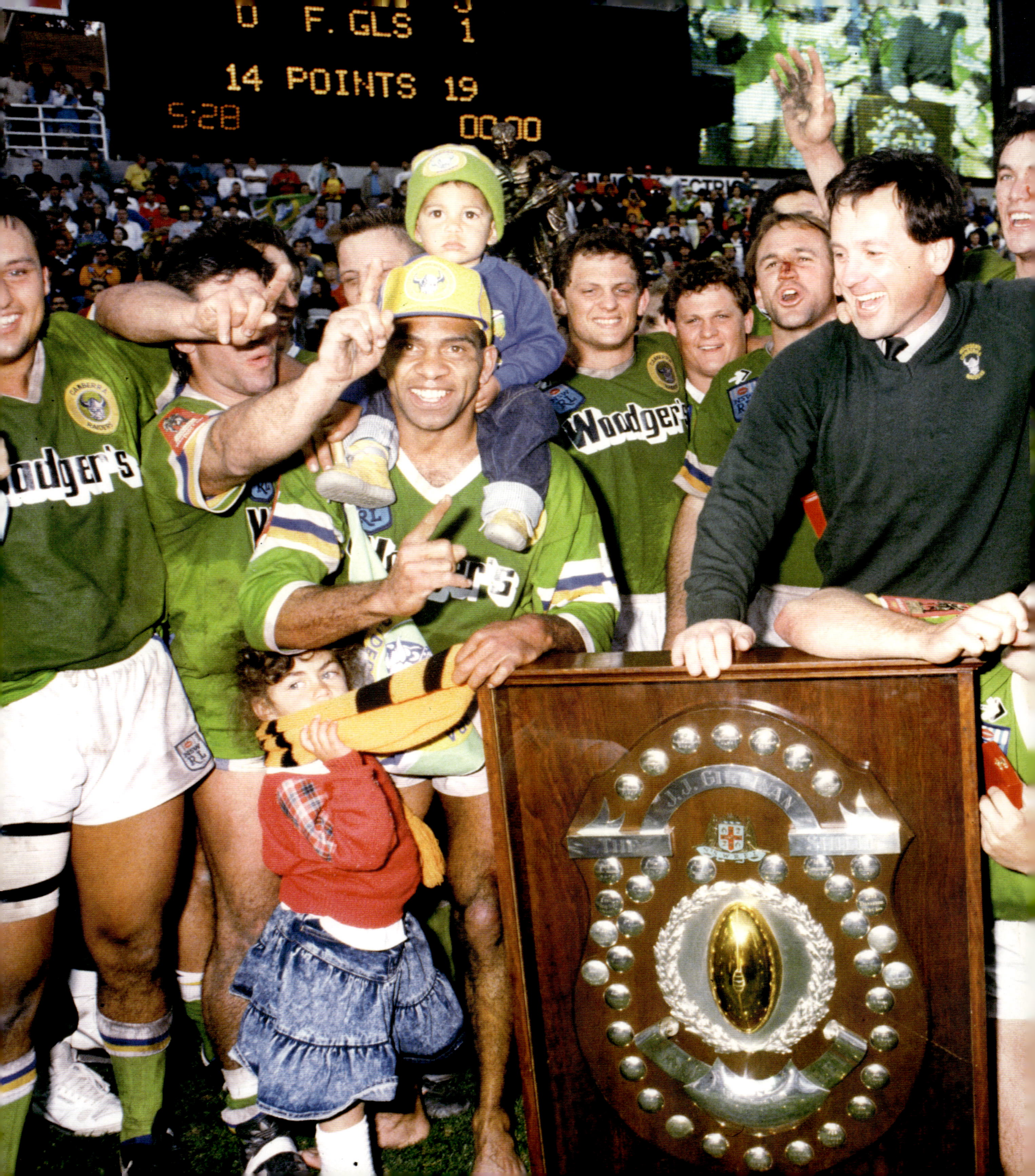
0 F. GLS 1
14 POINTS 19
5:28
00:00
Woodger's

110 YEARS OF RUGBY LEAGUE | **THE CLUBS**

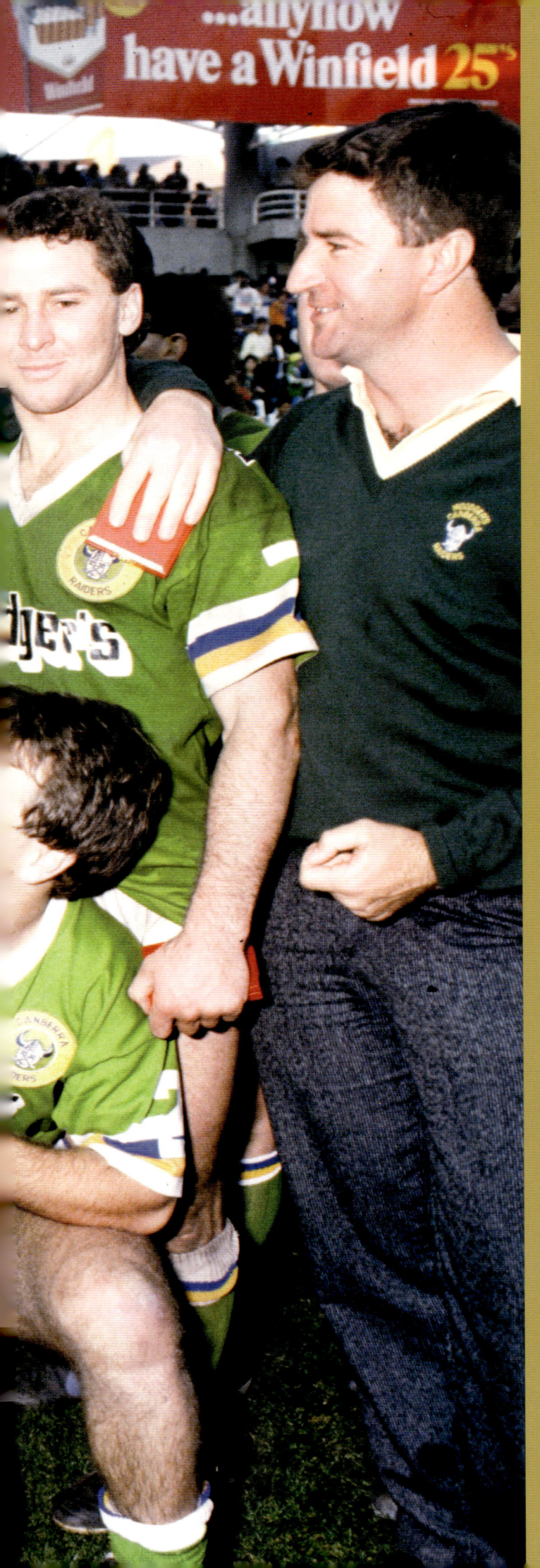

The 1989 decider between Canberra's Green Machine and the Balmain Tigers has gone down as one of the best Grand Finals ever played. The sides were locked 14-all after 80 minutes and the match went to extra-time. When the dust had finally settled it was Canberra celebrating a maiden title and Balmain rueing what might have been.

75

110 YEARS OF RUGBY LEAGUE | **THE CLUBS**

Arthur 'Pony' Halloway played 10 Tests for Australia between 1908-19 and led Balmain to four premierships as captain-coach.

Sweet taste of victory: Wally Lewis copped plenty of stick from the Parramatta Stadium crowd after Brisbane had defeated Illawarra 22-20 in the 1989 Amco Cup final. As was so often the case, The King had the last laugh.

Timing is everything in sport. And on the night of October 4, 2015 as the Cowboys basked in the glory of a maiden premiership, the NRL's lead photographer Grant Trouville got his timing right to the split second. Just as Johnathan Thurston had been in the zone when his moment arrived to ice the win in golden point, so, too, Trouville was at the top of his game when JT and daughter Frankie shared this touching moment in the centre of ANZ Stadium. An hour after the final siren, Thurston moved to the fence where his wife Samantha and their two daughters were standing. "Johnathan took Frankie and started to walk out the back of the media scrum and I walked next to him and congratulated him," Trouville reveals. "We walked to the middle of the field together and no one followed us so I had about 20-30 seconds on my own standing next to JT and Frankie. They were sitting on the ground and she grabbed his medal and they smiled at each other and before everyone else came over I had my shot." Trouville then had to make sure his iconic photo got to the NRL digital team quickly enough to be the lead photo on their full-time post. "They had a photo of Kyle Feldt ready to go but when I browsed back through my frames and realised what I had, I sprinted to the tunnel where the digital guys were about to press 'send' and I yelled out 'wait'," he says. And it's a good thing they did, because the shot of JT and Frankie would be viewed a staggering 12 million times within the next 24 hours.

78

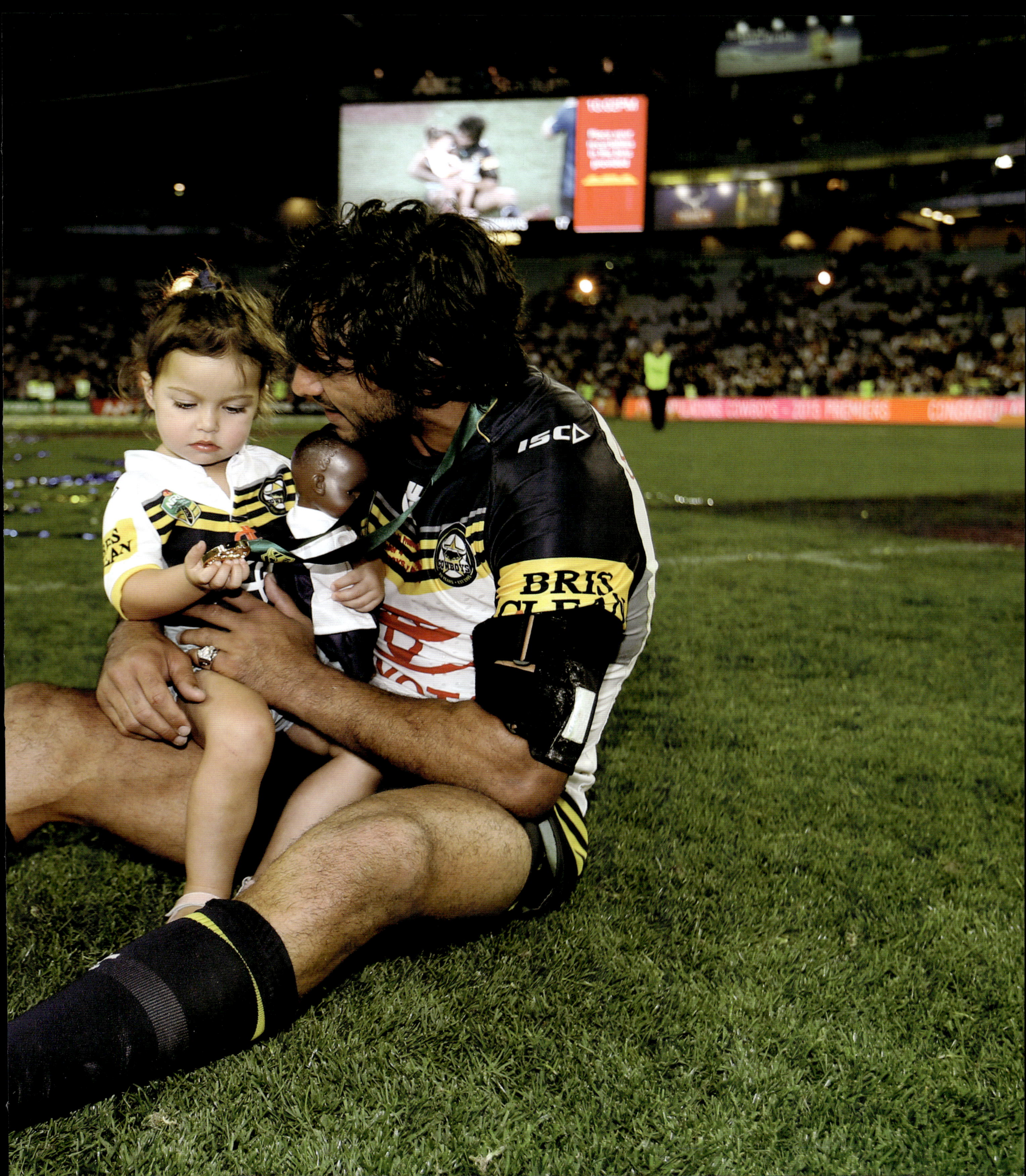
ISC
BRIS CLEAN

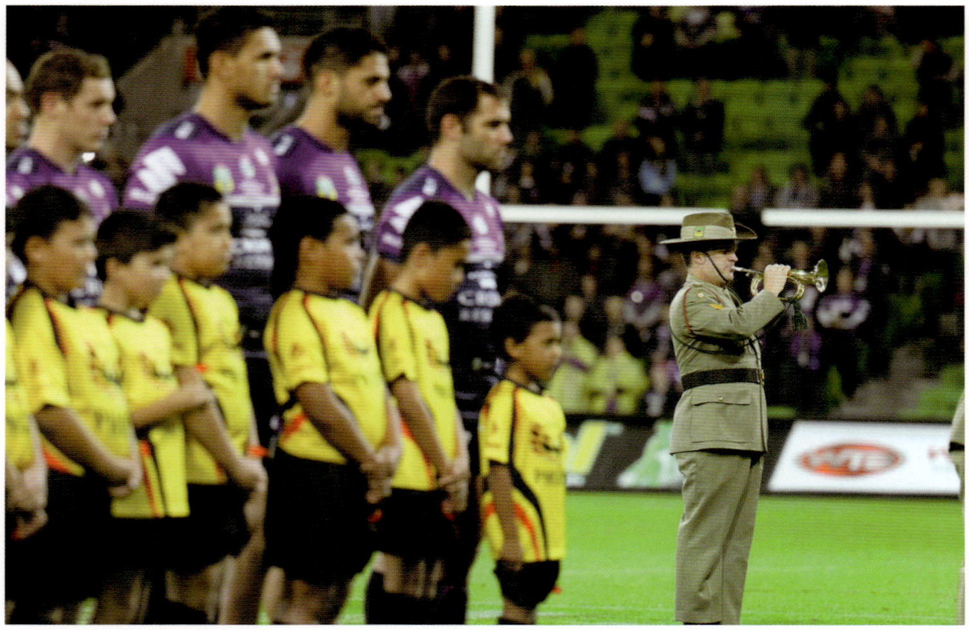

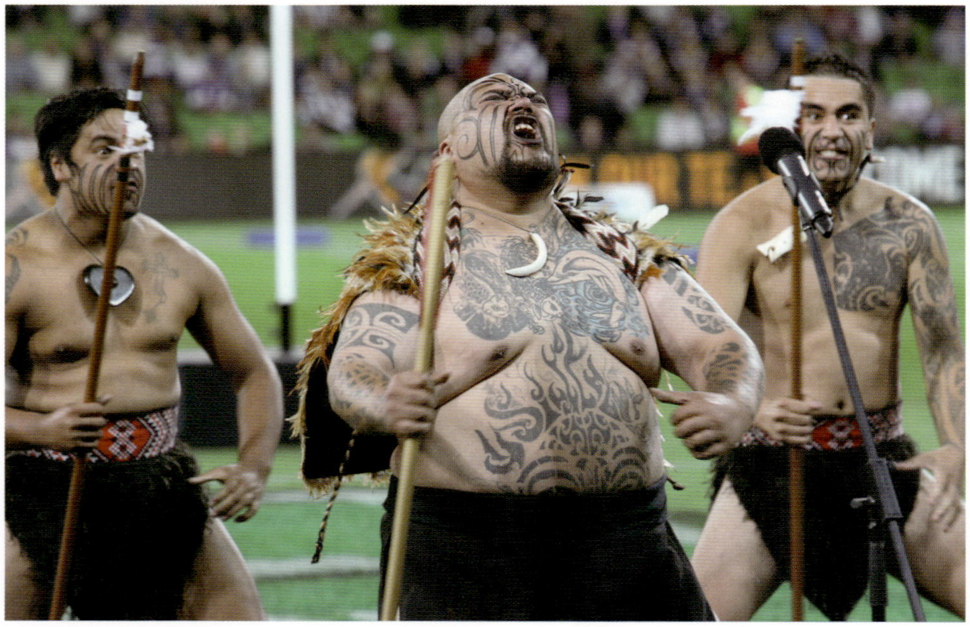

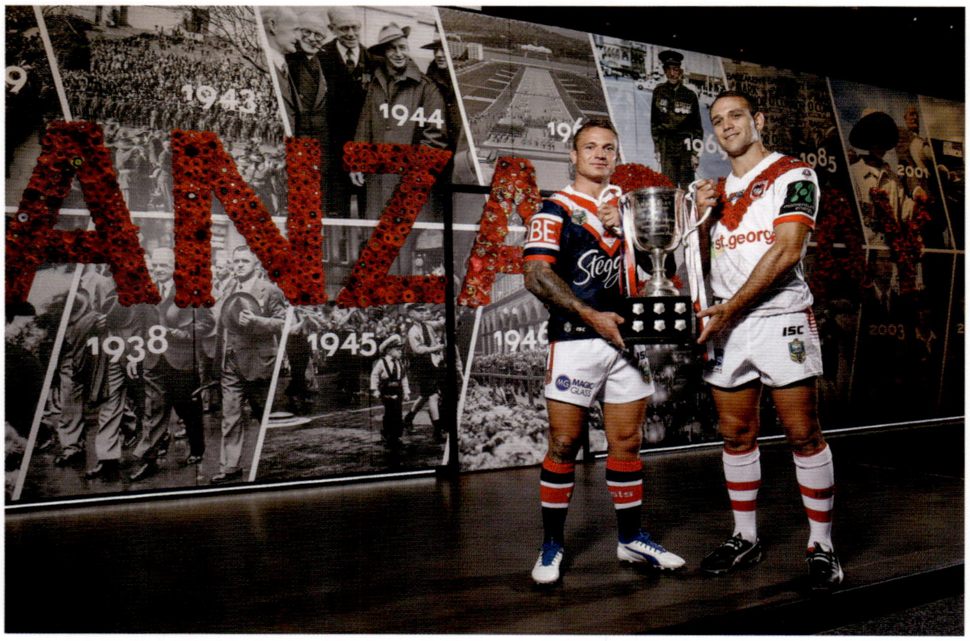
ANZA
1943
1944
1938
1945

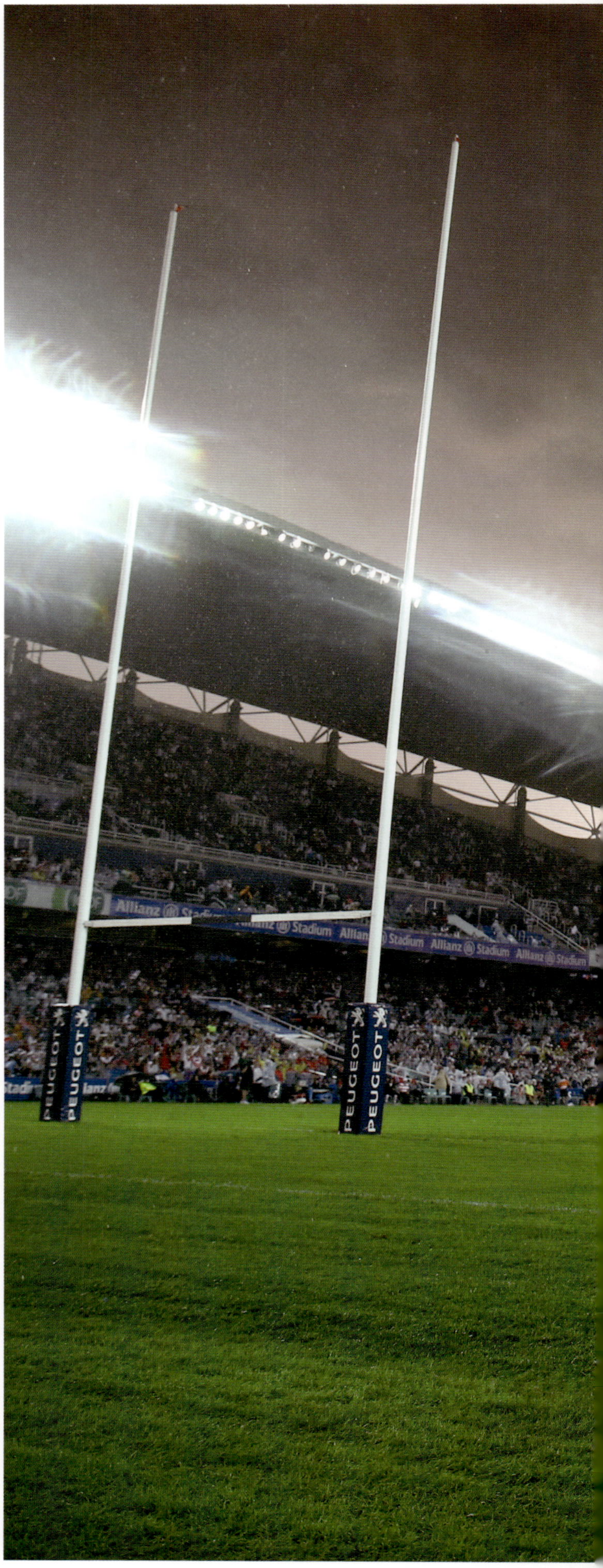
Allianz Stadium
PEUGEOT
PEUGEOT

110 YEARS OF RUGBY LEAGUE | **THE CLUBS**

Anzac Day has become one of the highlights of the NRL season – a day packed with emotion as we pay tribute to the men and women who served our nation in the field of war and then settle back to watch the Dragons and Roosters slug it out in Sydney and the Storm and Warriors clash in Melbourne. At Allianz Stadium in 2015 (main photo) the heavens opened in spectacular fashion and the players were forced to leave the field. When they returned it was the Red V who prevailed in another epic Anzac Day showdown.

81

No place for the faint hearted on Grand Final day 2012 as the Storm and Bulldogs exchanged pleasantries. Somewhere in the middle of all this is Dogs prop James Graham chomping on Billy Slater's ear – an unsavoury act which resulted in a 12-match ban for the Brit.

KooGa
CROWN
SUZUKI
doltone house
Jaycar Electronics
5
autObarn
doltone house
Jaycar Electronics
4
6
Jaycar
17
autObarn

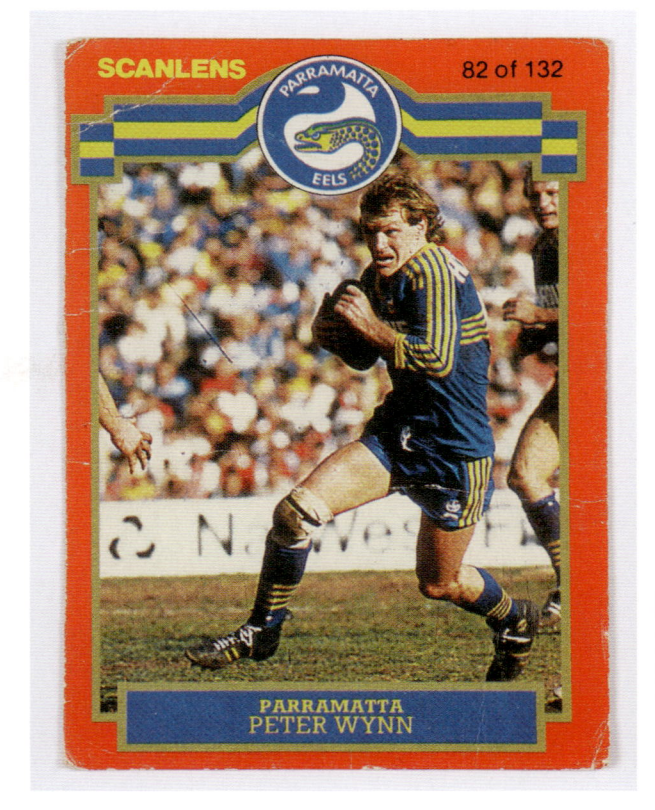

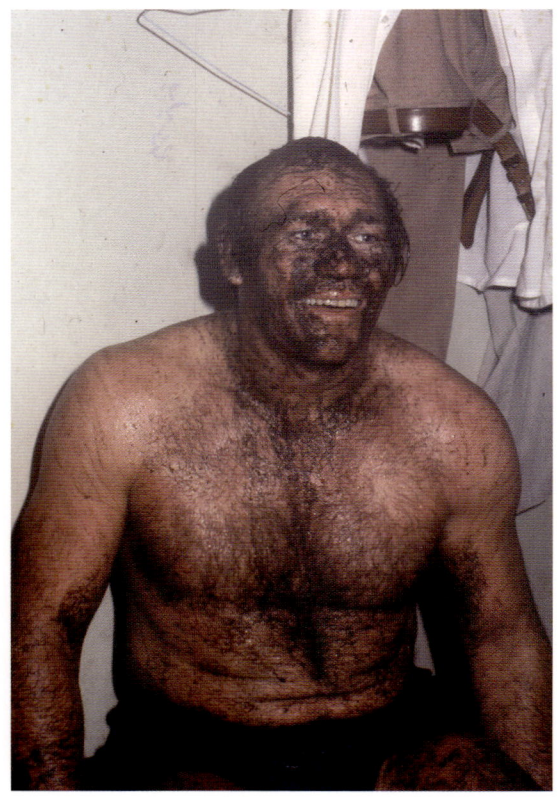

Triple treat: Steve Edge's inspirational leadership took Parra to the promised land in 1981, '82 and '83, getting the best out of young guns like Brett Kenny and Peter Sterling and old hands like Bob O'Reilly (left) who was lured out of retirement by Jack Gibson in 1981 and led from the front.

110 YEARS OF RUGBY LEAGUE | THE CLUBS

Nothing could faze 'The Guru' Eric Grothe, who would chill out before a game and then unleash his power on opposition defenders who were powerless to stop him.

Legend has it that Supercoach Jack Gibson's wife Judy hated his trademark fur coat but it certainly proved a lucky charm on rugby league's biggest stage.

110 YEARS OF RUGBY LEAGUE | THE CLUBS

The North Sydney Bears became extinct in 1999, but not before blokes like Peter Jackson and Mario Fenech played their way into the hearts of fans with their passion and pride.

Send the stretcher: Gregg Lennon is down for the count as a pair of North Sydney trainers stare forlornly into the distance in search of help.

A favourite son signs off: Robbie Farah gave his all for the Wests Tigers for more than a decade, and was part of the club's 2005 premiership. A falling out with coach Jason Taylor in 2015 saw Farah end his Tigers career in reserve grade but he wasn't going to miss one last farewell to the Leichhardt Oval faithful. On September 4, 2016, Farah watched on as the NRL side was flogged by the Raiders and then grabbed a beer and climbed the old scoreboard to reflect on his achievements.

PEARCE HILL

FAZZ + DEANO
TIGERS
LEGENDS
UP THE TIGERS
#YNWA 247

2040
4 EVER

Expansion arrived in a big way in 1995, with the addition of four new clubs taking the ARL to a whopping 20-team competition. All of a sudden, Queensland had three teams instead of one, and Steve Renouf's Broncos had company from Mario Fenech's South Queensland Crushers and Dean Schifilliti's North Queensland Cowboys. Aussie rock legend Billy Thorpe got in on the action for a promo.

Ken 'Arko' Arthurson was a player and coach at Manly before becoming club secretary in 1963 and overseeing a period of great success for the Sea Eagles. Arthurson would go on to serve as ARL chairman from 1984-97, before the Super League War took its toll and he stepped aside.

110 YEARS OF RUGBY LEAGUE | **THE CLUBS**

Making the '80s their own: the Bulldogs took home the title four times during a decade in which the names Mortimer, Lamb, Langmack, Johnstone and Folkes became synonymous with success. Sadly, the league world farewelled Steve Folkes (far right) in 2018 at the age of just 59.

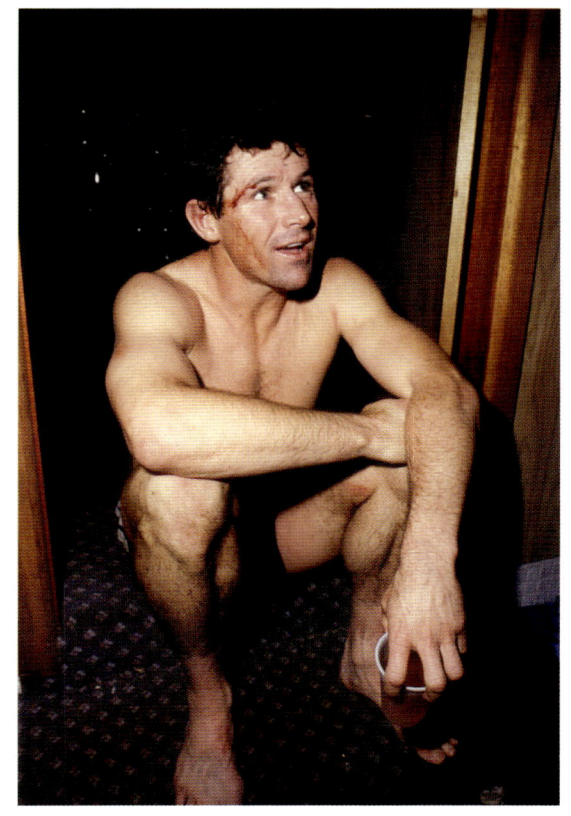

91

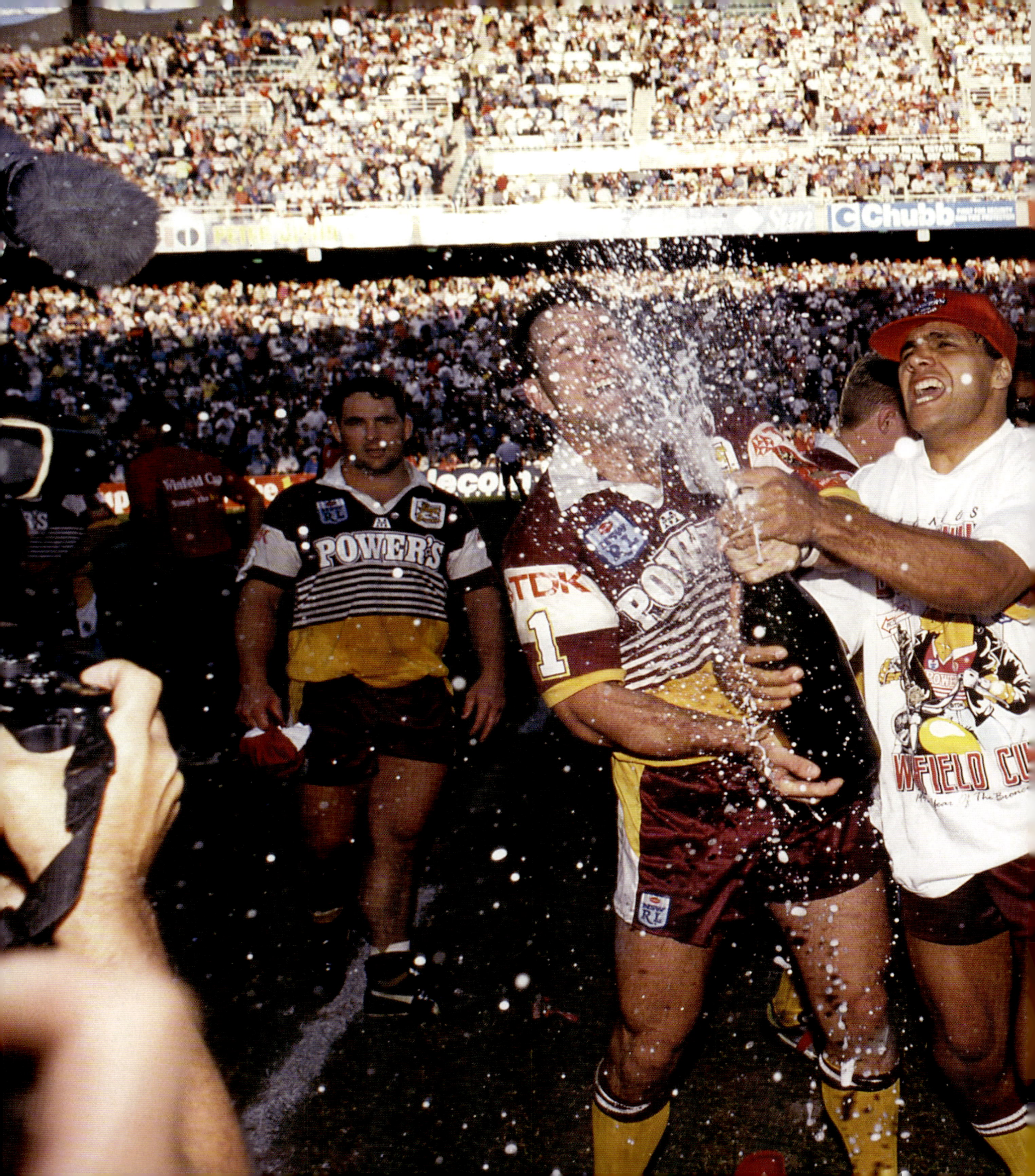
Chubb
POWER'S
TDK

They came, they saw, they conquered: Steve Renouf, Julian O'Neill and a posse of brilliant Broncos stormed Sydney in 1992-93 to take home back-to-back Winfield Cups.

110 YEARS OF RUGBY LEAGUE | THE CLUBS

Jillaroos stars Kezie Apps and Sam Bremner are St George Illawarra ambassadors and ready to play their part in the historic debut season of the NRL women's competition.

What better way for coach Michael Maguire to celebrate the Rabbitohs' first premiership in 43 years than with a Powerade shower.

'Leave it to Beaver'. Steve Menzies signed off in 2008 after an incredible career in which he surpassed Frank Burge as the top tryscoring forward of all-time. The much-loved Menzies got the perfect farewell when Manly smashed the Melbourne Storm in the 2008 Grand Final.

The Eagles Angels were formed in 2002, the brainchild of radio personality Wendy Harmer (third from left) and Sarah Murdoch. The pioneering female supporter group raised huge amounts of money for the club to help keep it afloat when times were tough. The Angels' members included surfing champ Layne Beachley (second from left), Olympic water polo gold medallist Debbie Watson (left), Olympic kayaker Naomi Flood (far right), Olympic sprinter Melinda Gainsford-Taylor and beach volleyball champ Kerri Pottharst. "It may well have been the first all-female corporate box in Australian sport, with our chandelier and soft wall paper," Harmer joked in an interview in 2015.

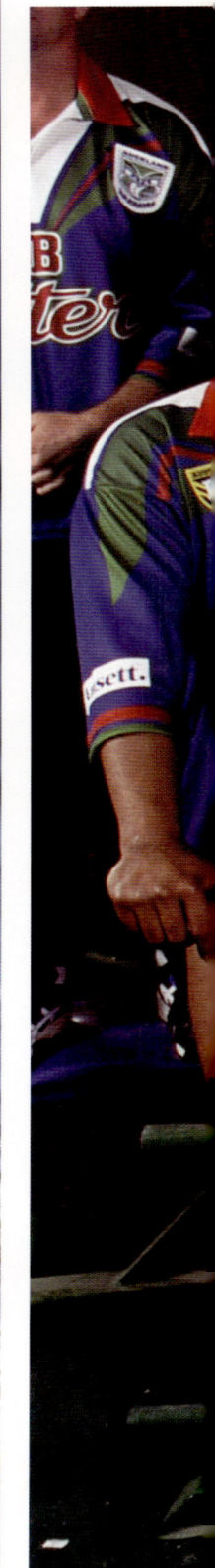

The Jones boy: Champion No.7 Stacey Jones played 261 games for the Warriors between 1995 and 2009, punching above his weight in every one of them and lifting all those around him.

110 YEARS OF RUGBY LEAGUE | **THE CLUBS**

The Auckland Warriors' entry into the Winfield Cup in 1995 was a massive shot in the arm for the game in New Zealand and the new boys showed they had what it took by winning six in a row mid-season.

110 YEARS OF RUGBY LEAGUE | **THE CLUBS**

Simply The Best: With Tina Turner's powerhouse songs as its anthem, rugby league's popularity soared in 1989-90 and Steve Roach and Marty Bella were only too happy to lend a hand.

Men of Steel: Collegians product Michael Bolt (left) played a club record 167 games for the Illawarra Steelers between 1982-90. Here he welcomes another local boy, Ken Daly, to first grade in 1986.

Flash Albert: With seven seconds remaining in the 1997 ARL decider between Newcastle and Manly, Darren Albert took a pass from Andrew Johns and raced into rugby league folklore as the Knights secured their first ever premiership.

110 YEARS OF RUGBY LEAGUE | **THE CLUBS**

Tears of joy for Panthers enforcer Mark Geyer after securing the club's first ever premiership in 1991. Big MG is joined by Ben Alexander, who sadly passed away just eight months later after a car accident. Just 20 at the time, Ben was the younger brother of club captain Greg Alexander.

110 YEARS OF RUGBY LEAGUE | THE CLUBS

Champers for the champs: Hard-nosed Englishman Kevin Ward (above) flew in from Castleford for the 1987 decider and proceeded to demolish the Canberra Raiders. Another bloke who knew what it took to get the job done on the big day was Harry Bath (right), who coached St George to Grand Final glory in 1977 and '79.

104

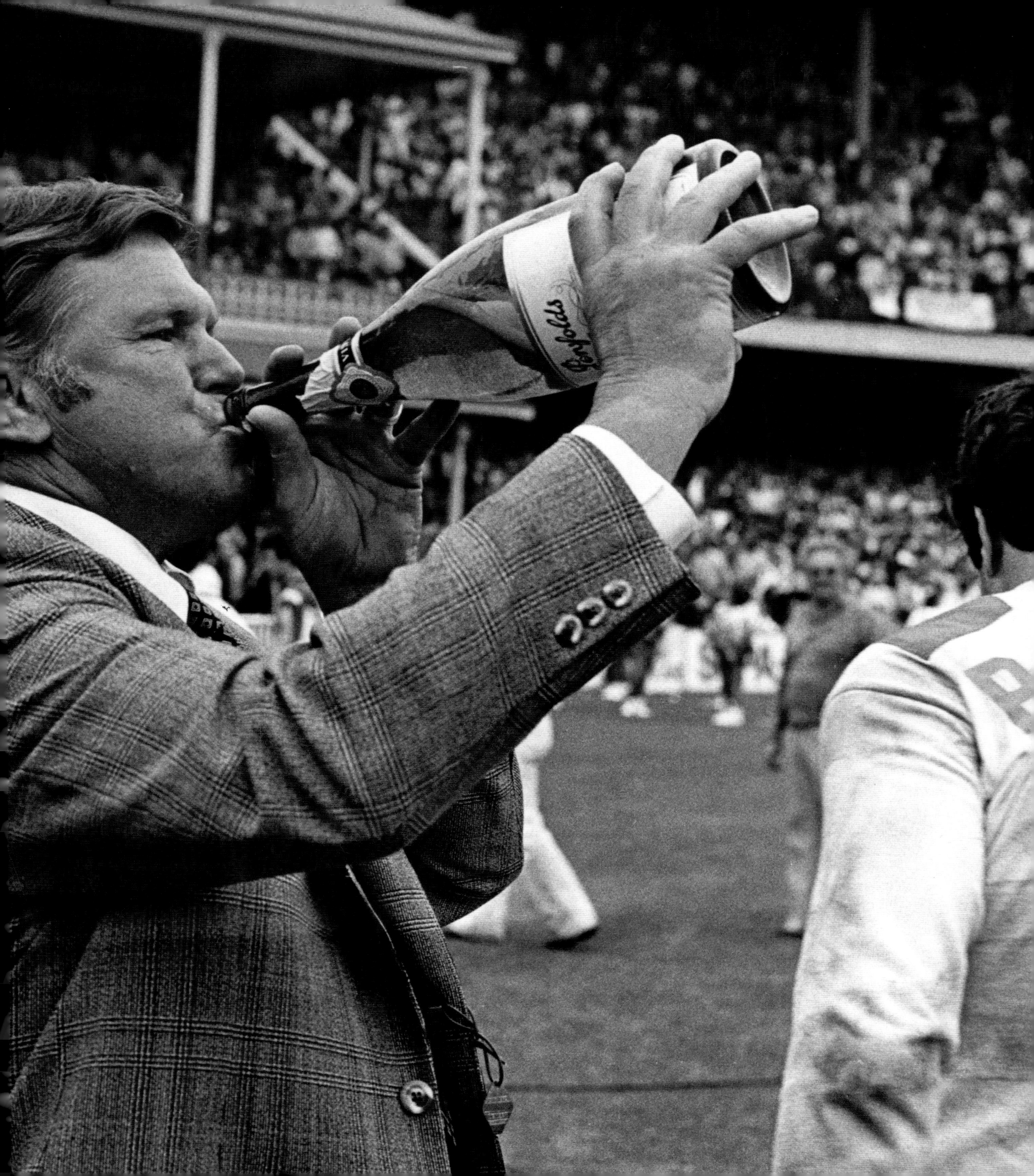
Penfolds

NOTICES TO ALL PLAYERS
TACKLE
TACKLE
TACKLE
AND
WIN

'Lord' Ted Goodwin could do outrageous things that others only dreamed of on a footy field but he also knew how to keep things simple.

110 YEARS OF RUGBY LEAGUE | **THE CLUBS**

You won't see a tackle like this in today's game but back in 1985 it was pretty much a case of anything goes — as Wynnum Manly's Bob Lindner found out when Ipswich got hold of him.

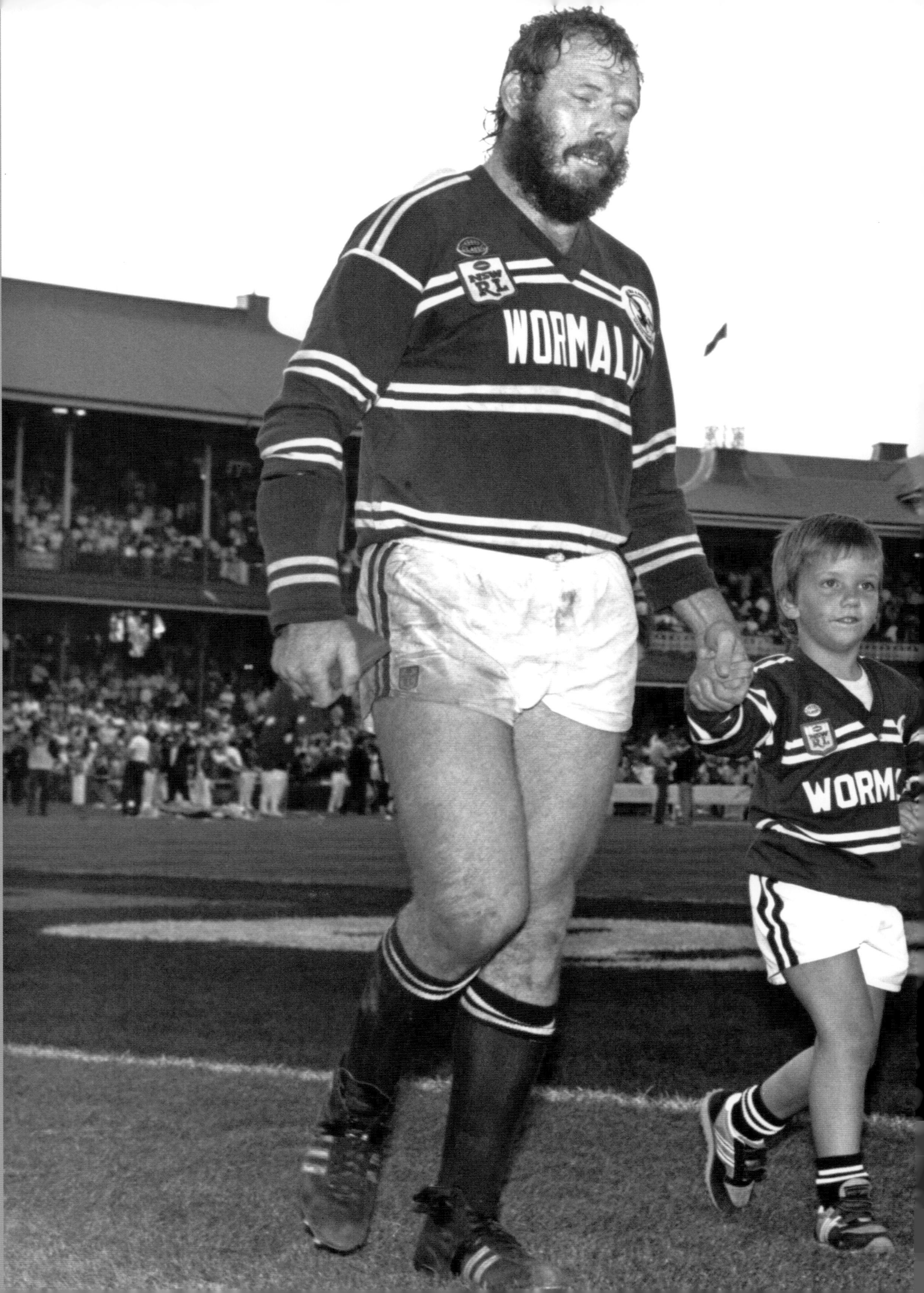
WORMALD
NSW RL
WORMA

110 YEARS OF RUGBY LEAGUE | **THE CLUBS**

The only thing better than winning a Grand Final is getting to share it with your family, and that's exactly what Manly powerhouse Noel Cleal did in 1987 when his sons Gareth and Kane joined him on the hallowed turf at the SCG.

109

THE KANGAROOS

What comes with achieving a dream is a responsibility to be a guardian of the culture and uphold the values of the green and gold.
— Darren Lockyer

110 YEARS OF RUGBY LEAGUE | THE KANGAROOS

From Australia's most-capped Kangaroo Darren Lockyer to men who donned the jersey just once, from the Little Master to Big Mal, and Wembley to Wellington, the honour of representing their country has had hearts racing and chests puffed out inside green and gold armour for more than a century.

From the very first Test match against Great Britain in 1908 through to the tense 6-0 triumph over England in the 2017 World Cup final, Australia's best and bravest have stood arm in arm to sing the national anthem before going into battle to do their nation proud.

By the end of that 2017 World Cup, Australia had taken the field 382 times in Test matches for a staggering 263 wins. Renowned for their flair, flamboyance and fierce will to win, the Kangaroos have taken on and taken down the finest the rugby league world has to offer.

For the mercurial Lockyer, whose record tally of 59 Test matches included 38 as captain, the milestones mean less than the mateship and memories.

"The first time you put that jersey on, it makes you reflect on the first time you laid eyes on it as a kid, which for me was watching the 1986 Kangaroos play in England," says Lockyer.

"There's the realisation that you are wearing a jersey that your childhood heroes wore. It's a surreal moment.

"In the early days when you went away on tour you only got one jersey, so it truly was something to treasure.

"It's not about what you're getting paid, it's the fact you represented the jersey, and there are a lot of people back home proud of what you did.

"A lot of my jerseys I wore in Tests, I never even washed. I just left them as they were when I walked off the field and wrote on the tags to remember which Test it was.

"They might be on the smelly side but they're more authentic. Different jerseys hold different memories so if it has a bit of grass on it from Elland Road or a bit of blood it makes it more special. A bit like Steve Waugh's baggy green."

That unwavering commitment to the jersey has seen countless men go above and beyond the call since 1908. Warriors like the late John O'Neill, a no-nonsense bushie who came to the big smoke to represent Souths, Manly and Australia with distinction in the '60s and '70s.

The man they called 'Lurch' was a big-game specialist, playing in nine Grand Finals and 10 Test matches, including the brutal 1970 World Cup final at Headingley in Leeds, won 12-7 by the Ron Coote-captained Kangaroos.

Coote's men were bashed and baited by the Brits but refused to buckle, with props O'Neill and Bob O'Reilly singled out for special attention.

O'Neill suffered a shocking cut to his shin but informed team-mates, 'I'll just keep my sock up and no one will notice'. These were the days before replacements, so leaving the field was simply not an option for Lurch, despite the fact his shinbone was clearly visible when he removed his sock after the match.

O'Neill also required stitches for a severe gash to his eye but the match had been won, the Kangaroos were on top of the world and his place in folklore was assured.

Another man to write his own part in Kangaroos history is 'The King', Wally Lewis.

As a wet-behind-the-ears 20-year-old in 1982, Lewis was part of the first Kangaroo touring side to go through England and France undefeated, earning the tag of 'The Invincibles'.

Four years later, as captain of his country, Lewis had the unenviable task of trying to emulate the deeds of that magnificent 1982 side.

Talk about pressure!

"Following in the footsteps of the '82 tour was as big a challenge as I ever had because we were on a hiding to nothing. If we won they'd say we only did what they did last time. If we got beaten they'd say we weren't as good as them," says Lewis, who captained Australia in 24 of his 34 Tests.

"Being part of those two tours taught me that there was a lot more to football and being a footballer than just winning the last game you played in.

"It wasn't just a record that we brought home for winning games. It was a camaraderie and friendships that will last a lifetime between an outstanding bunch of blokes who enjoyed life away from football as well.

"And when they blew full-time in the last game of the tour in France and we'd managed to win every game again, I just felt a great relief. I matured a hell of a lot on that tour in terms of captaincy and the importance of realising you weren't just there as part of a Contiki tour. We were there as footballers first, second and third."

And in the great Kangaroo tradition, bloody good footballers at that.

Darren Lockyer is given a guard of honour by teammates after his final Test match on home soil, a 42-6 thrashing of the Kiwis in Newcastle in October, 2011.

A glorious night for Australian rugby league on December 2, 2017 at Suncorp Stadium as Cameron Smith's Australians took out the World Cup for the 11th time. Melbourne's Will Chambers (left) was overcome with emotion while Blues brothers David Klemmer and Aaron Woods celebrated in typically unique style.

110 YEARS OF RUGBY LEAGUE | **THE KANGAROOS**

The women's World Cup Final was played for the first time as a curtain-raiser to the men's final and the Australian Jillaroos stormed to victory over arch-rivals New Zealand, much to the delight of Ruan Sims and Kezie Apps.

110 YEARS OF RUGBY LEAGUE | **THE KANGAROOS**

The 1982 Invincibles: (left to right) Steve Mortimer, Ray Price, Steve Ella, Brett Kenny, Wally Lewis, Ian Schubert and Kerry Boustead raise a glass to a history-making tour.

Standing proud: (left to right) Craig Young, Wayne Pearce, Rod Reddy, Les Boyd, Ray Price, Eric Grothe, Mal Meninga, Brett Kenny and Kerry Boustead prepare to go into battle.

116

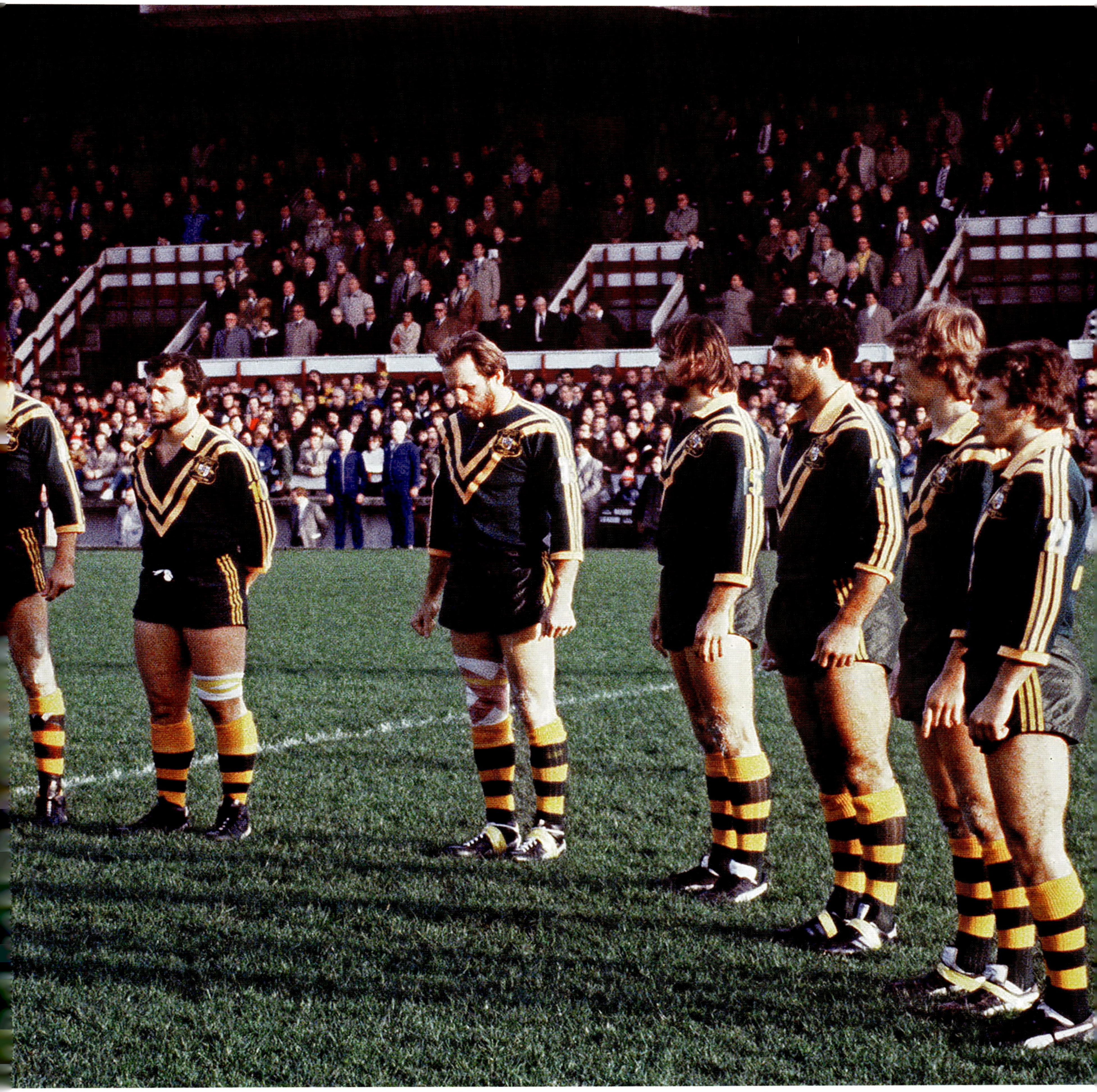

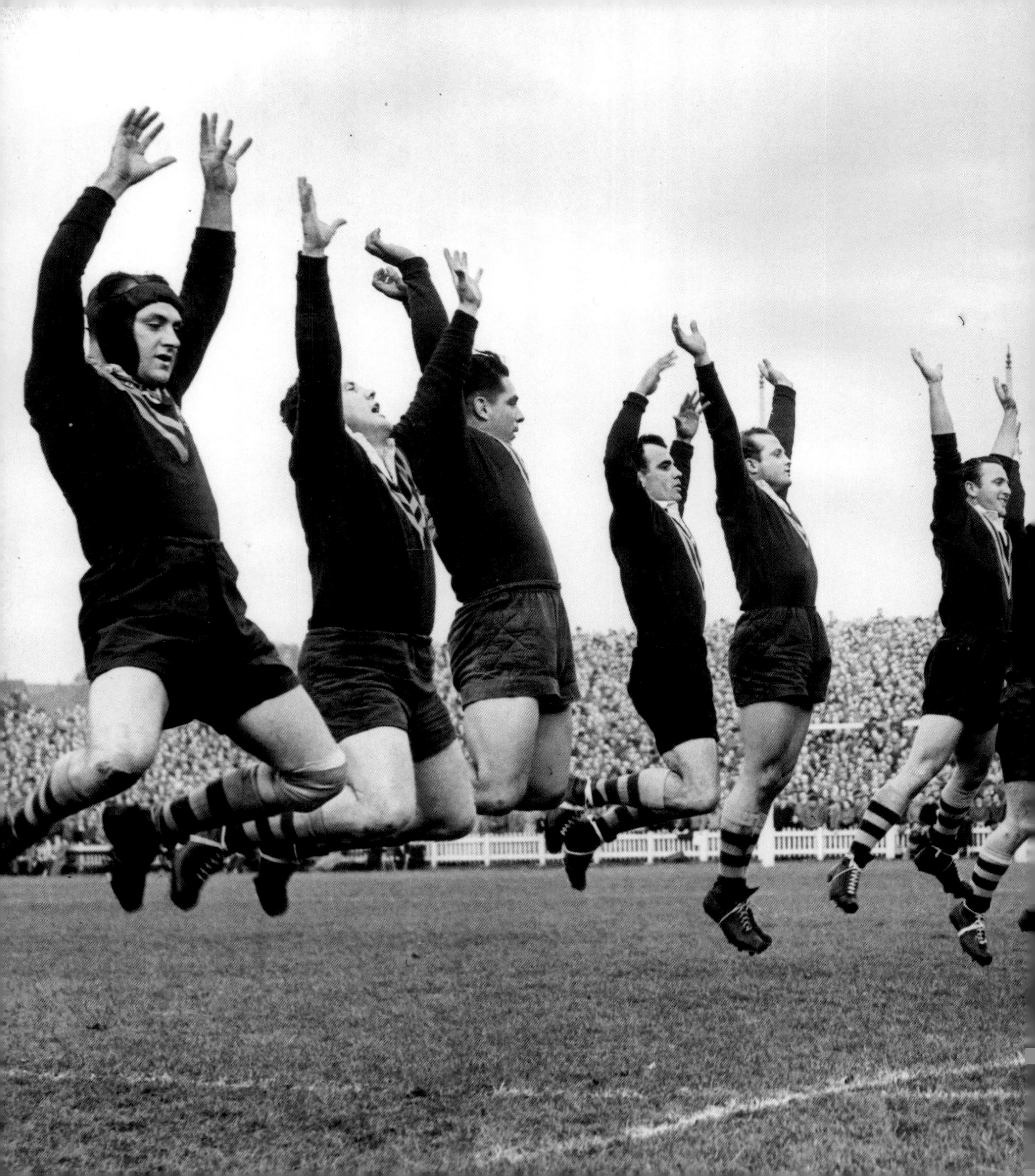

Leap of faith: the 1952 Kangaroos included such famous names as Clive Churchill, Duncan Hall, Brian Davies and Ferris Ashton, all of whom were happy to rip out a full-blooded war cry before taking on the British.

110 YEARS OF RUGBY LEAGUE | **THE KANGAROOS**

Room for one more? The Kangaroos squads of 1948 (right) and 1952 (above) found it tough going on the field against the old enemy Great Britain but their bond was unbreakable and they did Australia proud.

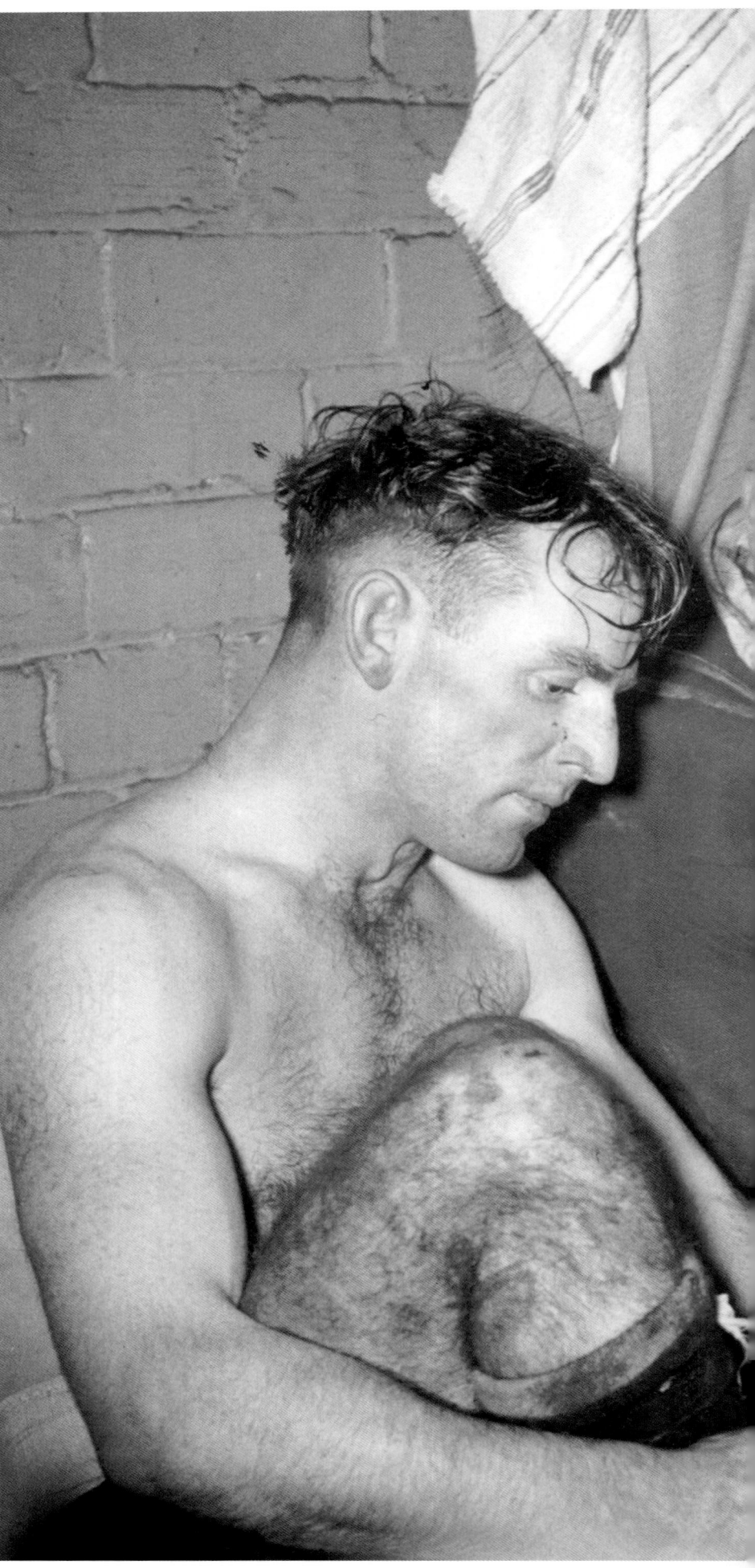

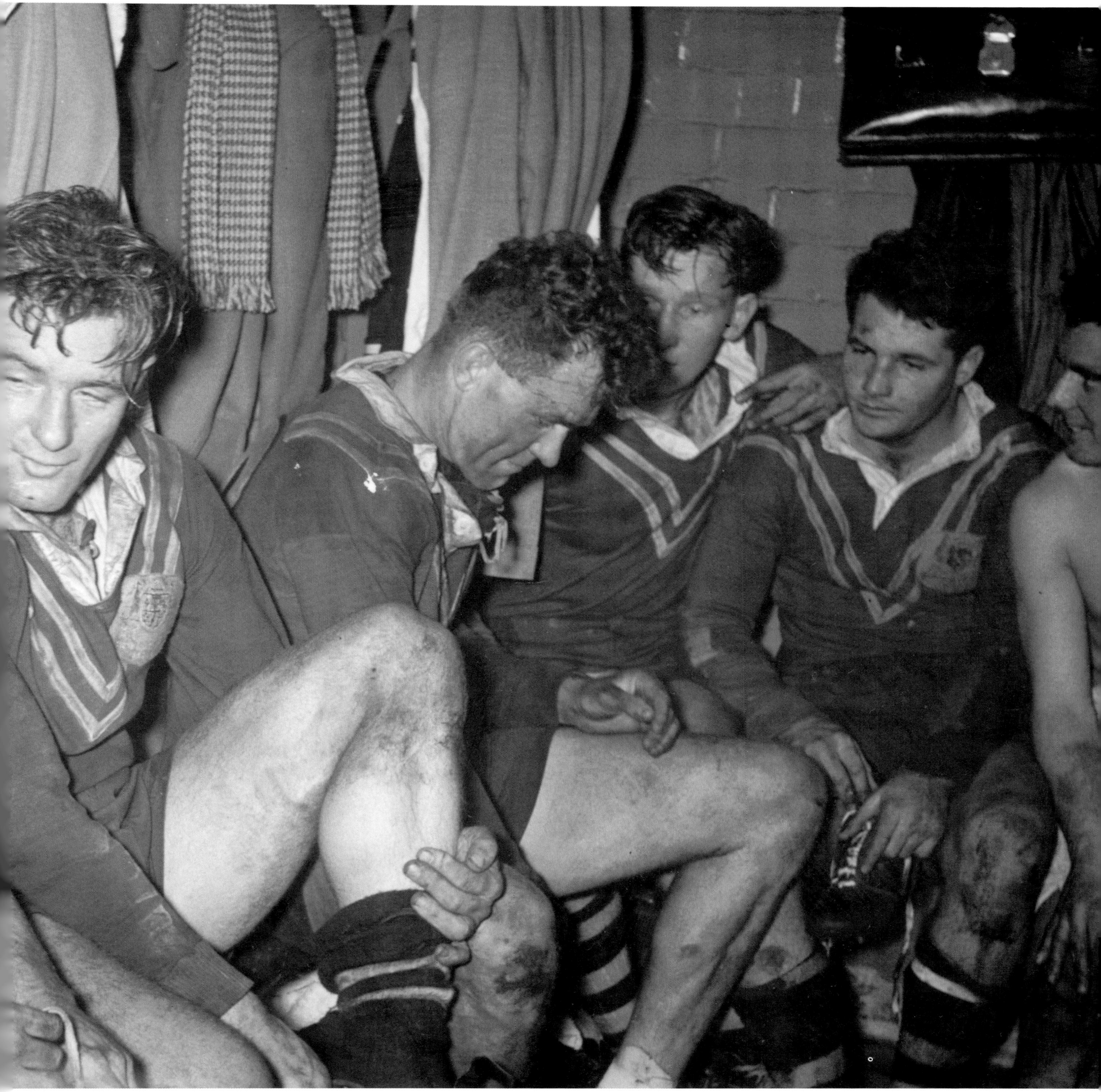

110 YEARS OF RUGBY LEAGUE | THE KANGAROOS

What happens on tour: Steve Roach plays Santa Claus in England in 1990 and Mal Meninga, the only man in history to go on four Kangaroo tours, takes a stroll with a local canine friend.

122

Is there anything Big Mal couldn't do? Here he completes running repairs on Kevin Walters' jersey as Allan Langer looks on.

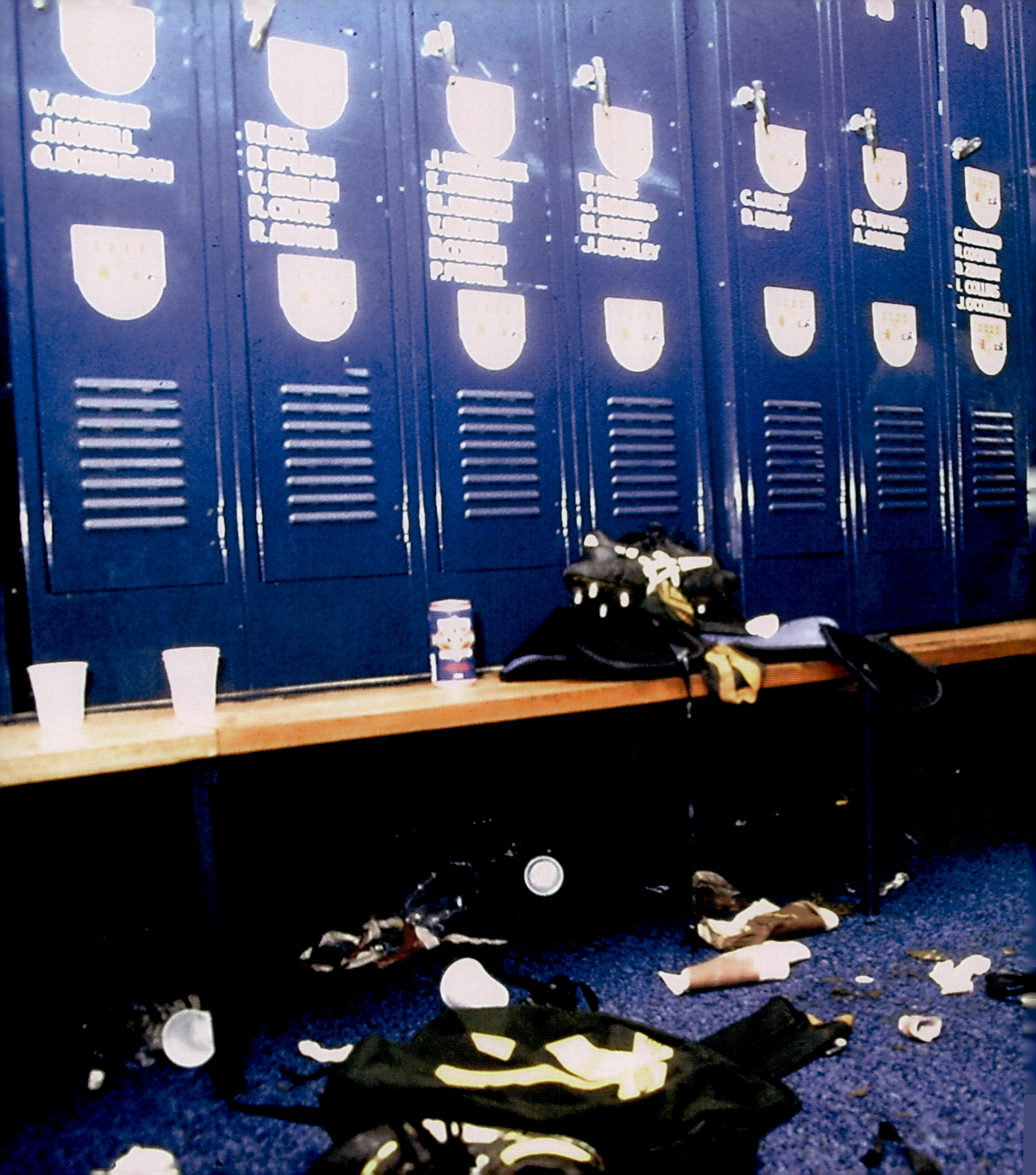

110 YEARS OF RUGBY LEAGUE | **THE KANGAROOS**

Allan Langer enjoys the sanctity of the Australian dressing room after giving his all for the Green and Gold. 'Alf' played 24 Tests for his country and was part of the 1990 and '94 Kangaroo tours.

AUSSIE, AUSSIE, AUSSIE!

BIGGEST TEST WIN
Australia **110-4** Russia
The Boulevard, Hull,
November 4, 2000

MOST POINTS IN A TEST
Ryan Girdler **46**
vs Russia @ The Boulevard, Hull,
November 4, 2000

MOST TRIES IN A TEST
Valentine Holmes **6**
vs Fiji @ Suncorp Stadium, Brisbane,
November 24, 2017

OLDEST TEST PLAYER
Sandy Pearce **38 years, 158 days**
vs England, November 5, 1921

YOUNGEST TEST PLAYER
Sione Mata'utia **18 years, 129 days**
vs England, November 2, 2014

The battle between Australia and Great Britain is as old as the game itself and has proved the ultimate testing ground for footy's finest. The Brits enjoyed some golden years in the 1940s and '50s but since 1977, Australia have lost to GB only eight times and England only once.

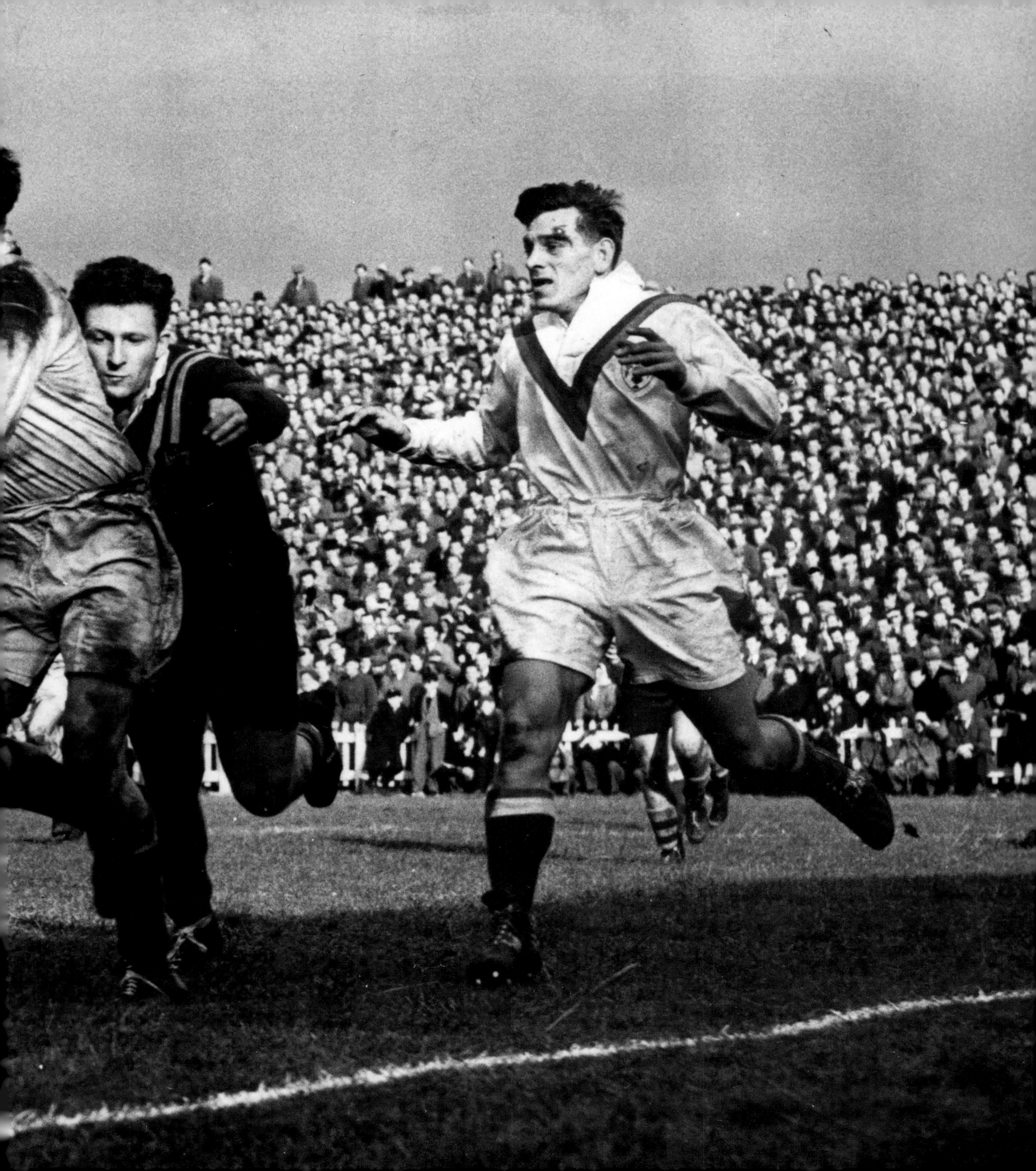

110 YEARS OF RUGBY LEAGUE | **THE KANGAROOS**

1952: Kangaroos skipper Clive Churchill and his Great Britain counterpart Willie Horne lead their teams out.

1982: Captain Max Krilich and coach Frank Stanton were at the helm of The Invincibles.

1992: World Cup glory for Bob Fulton, Mal Meninga and Ken Arthurson.

128 Ken

Captain Cam: Having led Australia to World Cup success in 2017, Cameron Smith entered 2018 on 56 Test appearances, just three behind Darren Lockyer's record of 59.

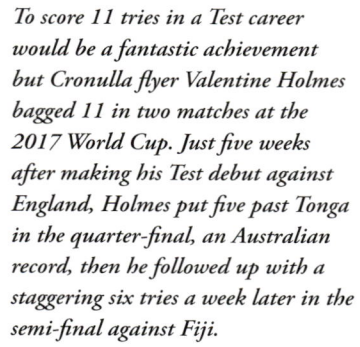

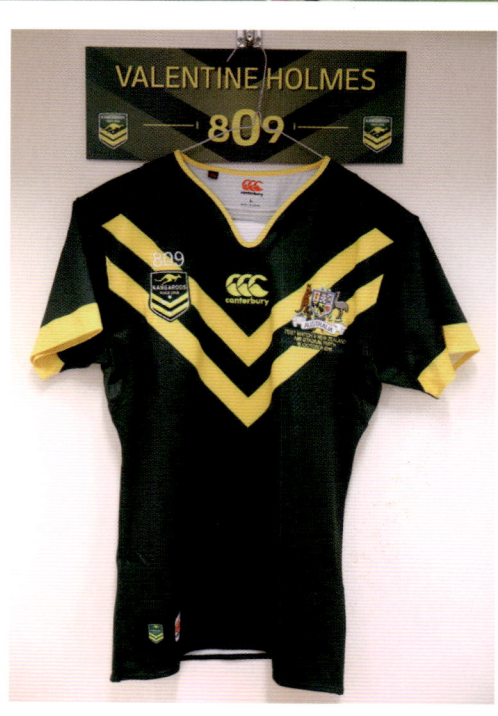

To score 11 tries in a Test career would be a fantastic achievement but Cronulla flyer Valentine Holmes bagged 11 in two matches at the 2017 World Cup. Just five weeks after making his Test debut against England, Holmes put five past Tonga in the quarter-final, an Australian record, then he followed up with a staggering six tries a week later in the semi-final against Fiji.

On top of the world: Valentine Holmes and Dane Gagai soak up the elation of Australia's gripping 6-0 win over England in the 2017 World Cup final in Brisbane.

Hanging off every word: Frank Stanton took charge of the Green and Gold in 26 Tests between 1978 and '84. His record was a phenomenal 23 wins and three losses, including the 1982 Invincibles tour, the first Kangaroos team to go through Great Britain and France unbeaten.

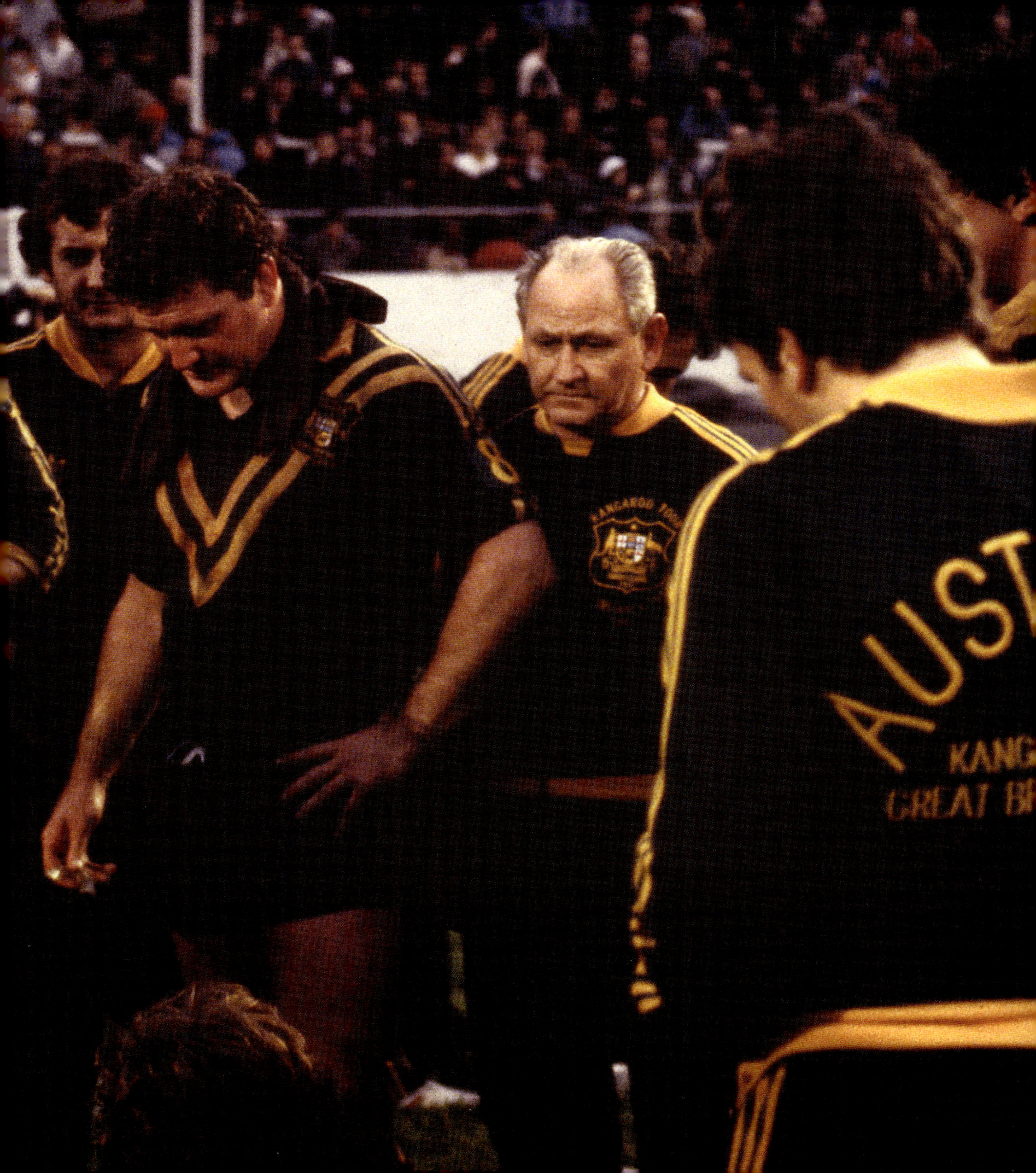
AUST
KANG
GREAT BR

Only four men in the history of the game have played more Tests for Australia than Petero Civoniceva, who turned out 45 times for his country and led from the front each and every time. The warhorse front-rower also played in two premiership-winning Brisbane Broncos teams, in 1998 and 2006.

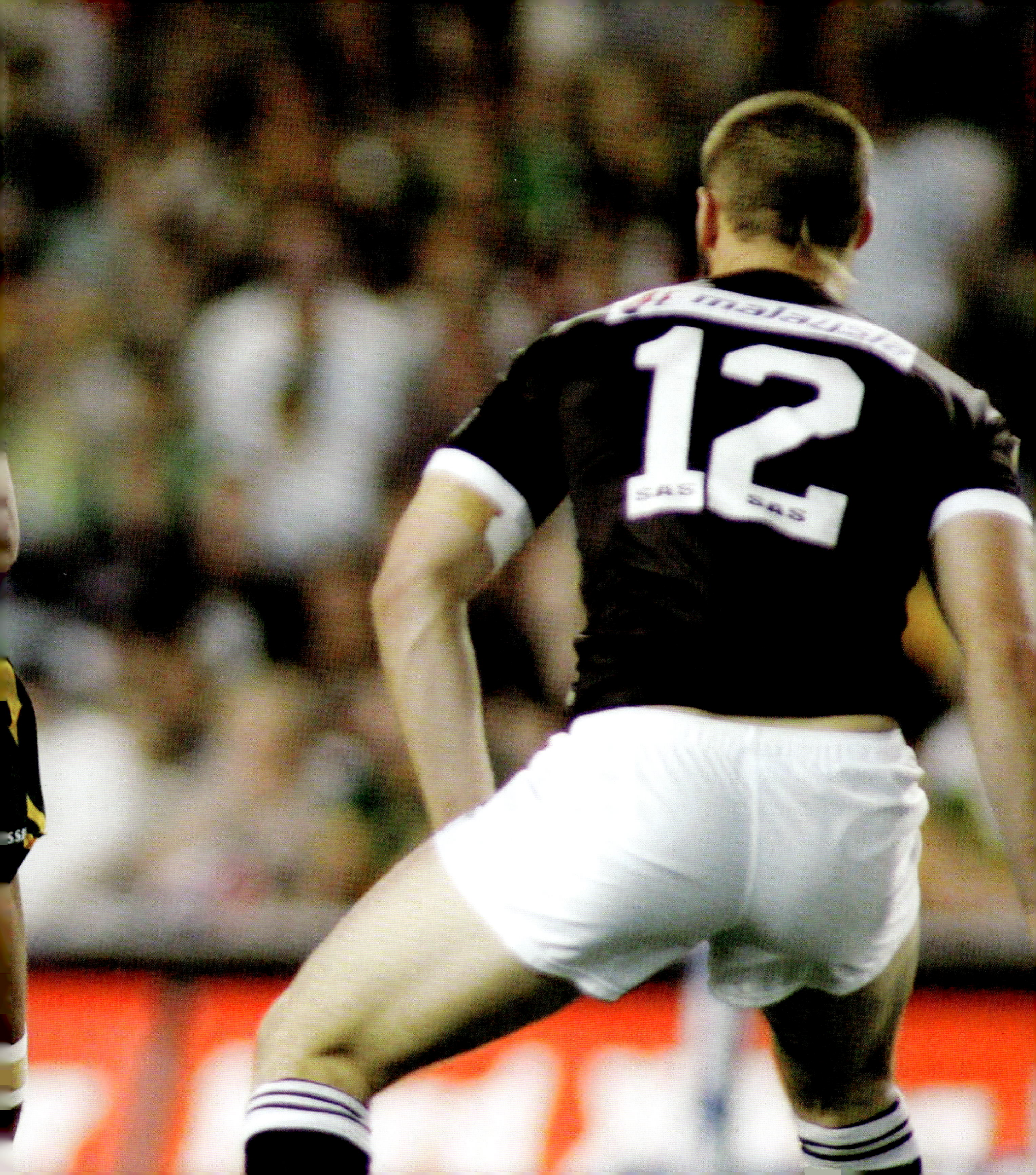
malaysia
12
SAS
SAS

Lang Park 1985 and rival hardmen Greg Dowling and Kevin Tamati slug it out on the wrong side of the white line as a Trans-Tasman Test turns ugly.

Captain-coached by Graeme Langlands, the 1973 Kangaroos boasted strikepower across the paddock. They won back the Ashes with a hard-fought 2-1 series triumph.

110 YEARS OF RUGBY LEAGUE | **THE KANGAROOS**

Signal of intent: Benji Marshall and the Kiwis put extra venom into their haka before the 2008 World Cup Final in Brisbane and then proceeded to stun the Australians 34-20. It was the Kiwis' first ever World Cup triumph and ended 33 years of Green and Gold domination of the tournament.

110 YEARS OF RUGBY LEAGUE | **THE KANGAROOS**

Let's party: Skipper Brad Fittler was inspirational as the Kangaroos downed England 16-8 in the 1995 World Cup Final at Wembley. Coach Bob Fulton labelled it the best win he'd seen since taking over as national coach in 1989.

The ultimate warrior, Ray Price, gave his heart and soul to the Aussie cause in 22 Tests between 1978 and '84.

Australian coach Mal Meninga has embraced the tradition of the national team and at the 2017 Kangaroos reunion at the SCG, he asked award-winning photographer Gregg Porteous to recreate a team photo of the 1908 Kangaroos, complete with blazers, caps and a kangaroo out front. With skipper Cameron Smith front and centre, the Australians look ready to take on the world . . . and beat them.

141

STATE OF ORIGIN

For the best part of four decades, three epic encounters each year have pitted two fierce interstate rivals against each other and one thing is certain . . . this means war.

110 YEARS OF RUGBY LEAGUE | STATE OF ORIGIN

If you were handing out awards for the bravest gamble in the game's history, visionaries Ron McAuliffe and Kevin Humphreys would stand side by side on the top step of the podium for a little concept they called State of Origin. After decades of NSW domination, interstate footy was on its knees. Queensland had won just four matches in 20 years and the heavy defeats were made even more galling by the fact that the Sunshine State's finest would pull on a blue jersey every year and turn on their own.

So bad had things become in 1980 that the players could have done a lap of dishonour at full time and met every fan in person when a paltry 1638 turned up for the meaningless second game of the interstate series at Leichhardt Oval.

Just six weeks later, on July 8, the game changed forever when a heaving mass of 33,210 Maroon fans turned up at Lang Park to see Ron and Kev's vision come to fruition. The third game of the 1980 series had been chosen as the Origin 'guinea pig' and few could have imagined the phenomenon it would become.

"Origin was desperately needed and you have to take your hat off to McAuliffe and Humphreys for having the presence of mind to recognise that," says Maroons great Chris Close, who was just 21 when he charged on to Lang Park that night. "It was a huge step and they must have been shaking in their boots to make such a bold move and then sell it to the doubters."

Suddenly Queensland's finest were wearing the right jersey and fighting for the right cause and they had the right man to lead them into battle – Arthur Beetson. He may have been 35 and past his prime but God help anyone who got in his way.

"I was lucky enough to have my bag beside Arthur's in the dressing room and I'll never forget the moment he put the war paint on and I looked at him and thought, 'this is a war, this isn't a normal part of your life'," Close recalls.

"He smothered his face in Vaseline and he had resin all over his jersey and arms – it was probably bloody poison – but his focus was clear. He wasn't a yeller or screamer and we didn't need to be told anyway. We knew this moment would define all of us.

"I often live that moment when I need to galvanise myself – we did it then so why can't we do it now? That was a valuable lesson in my life to know that regardless of the task and the adversity you face, there is always a way through it.

"If you can gather your energy and muster it all like Artie showed us that night, then there's nothing that can beat us."

Certainly not NSW that night, as the Maroons stormed to an emotion-charged 20-10 win on the back of a rampaging Close try, Mal Meninga's radar boot and Beetson's sheer bloody-mindedness. It set the tone for a period of Queensland dominance that would last five years until the Blues found an inspirational leader of their own to turn back the tide.

Steve 'Turvey' Mortimer was a veteran of eight Tests, a Kangaroo tour and premiership triumphs with Canterbury in 1980 and '84. But for all the highs, Mortimer had suffered the pain of three series losses at Origin level and he'd had a gutful. The renaissance began in the third game of the '84 series when Mortimer was handed the captaincy of a NSW team featuring six debutants, including his brother Chris, Peter Wynn, Steve Morris and Brian Johnston.

The Blues won that match 22-12 at a hostile Lang Park, laying the foundations for their drought-breaking triumph in 1985.

"I had grown up with my brothers dreaming of putting on the sky blue jersey, as any proud New South Welshman would," says Mortimer. "We won the first game at Lang Park in '85 and then went to the SCG to try and finish the job in front of our own people. The feeling when Brett Kenny crossed to wrap up that second game was pure joy. I collapsed to the ground and kissed the turf and thanked God for the opportunity to make history for NSW. It was a moment that changed my life."

Such is the power of Origin that it has continued changing lives for 33 more years – and will likely do so for the next 33. For kids like Ben Ikin and Brad Fittler and Brett Dallas, who all debuted as 18-year-olds in the game's most demanding arena. For Trevor Gillmeister, who rose from his hospital bed in 1995 to help Paul Vautin's underdogs complete a 3-0 series sweep. For Meninga, who was there on night one, and would stand like a colossus in the Origin arena 32 times as a player and 30 more times as a coach as he led Queensland to nine series wins. For the ultimate Blueblood Laurie Daley, who savoured a trifecta of series wins as a captain in 1992, '93 and '94 and then two decades later coached the NSW side that ended eight years of Maroon domination.

For Immortal Wally Lewis, who captained his state 30 times and still gets shivers down the spine when he recalls the bravery of his men in Game Two, 1989, when they defied an outrageous injury toll to prevail 16-12 in enemy territory.

Lewis takes up the story: "Bob Lindner kept saying, 'my leg's sore, I need to go off', but I just told him to keep going because we'd already lost Mal with a fractured cheekbone, Langer with a broken leg and Vautin with a dislocated elbow.

"Finally with about seven minutes to go, Lindner couldn't do it any more and he went off . . . turns out he had a broken leg!

"I think it's the only game in Origin history where a team has left the field without the full number of players.

"We went into sheds and Artie was crying. He said it was the gutsiest thing he had ever seen from a footy team. For the players to have a legend of the game give them the biggest rap they'd ever had in their lives, they'll never forget that."

And that's the magic of Origin.

Arthur Beetson leads his men on to Lang Park in 1980. Rival captain Tommy Raudonikis would later admit, 'Artie's eyes were rolling in his head and he was frothing at the mouth. It was scary'.

1985: Steve Mortimer and the moment that changed his life.

1995: Adrian Lam, Mark Coyne, Wayne Bartrim and Gavin Allen celebrate after Paul Vautin's underdogs had pulled off a stunning upset.

Allan Langer and Paul Vautin had plenty of company in the Maroons' sick bay during Game Two of 1989 but somehow Queensland defied the odds to record a famous win.

Tezza and Tallis go toe-to-toe: Taken by Col Whelan, this remains one of the finest Origin snaps ever taken, summing up perfectly how much it means to the players. Two of the game's fiercest competitors, Terry Hill and Gorden Tallis, squared off in Game Two of the 1999 series and neither was prepared to back down. As Hill told Rugby League Week in 2005, "Tallis had been dominating Origin for years and someone had to stand up to him".

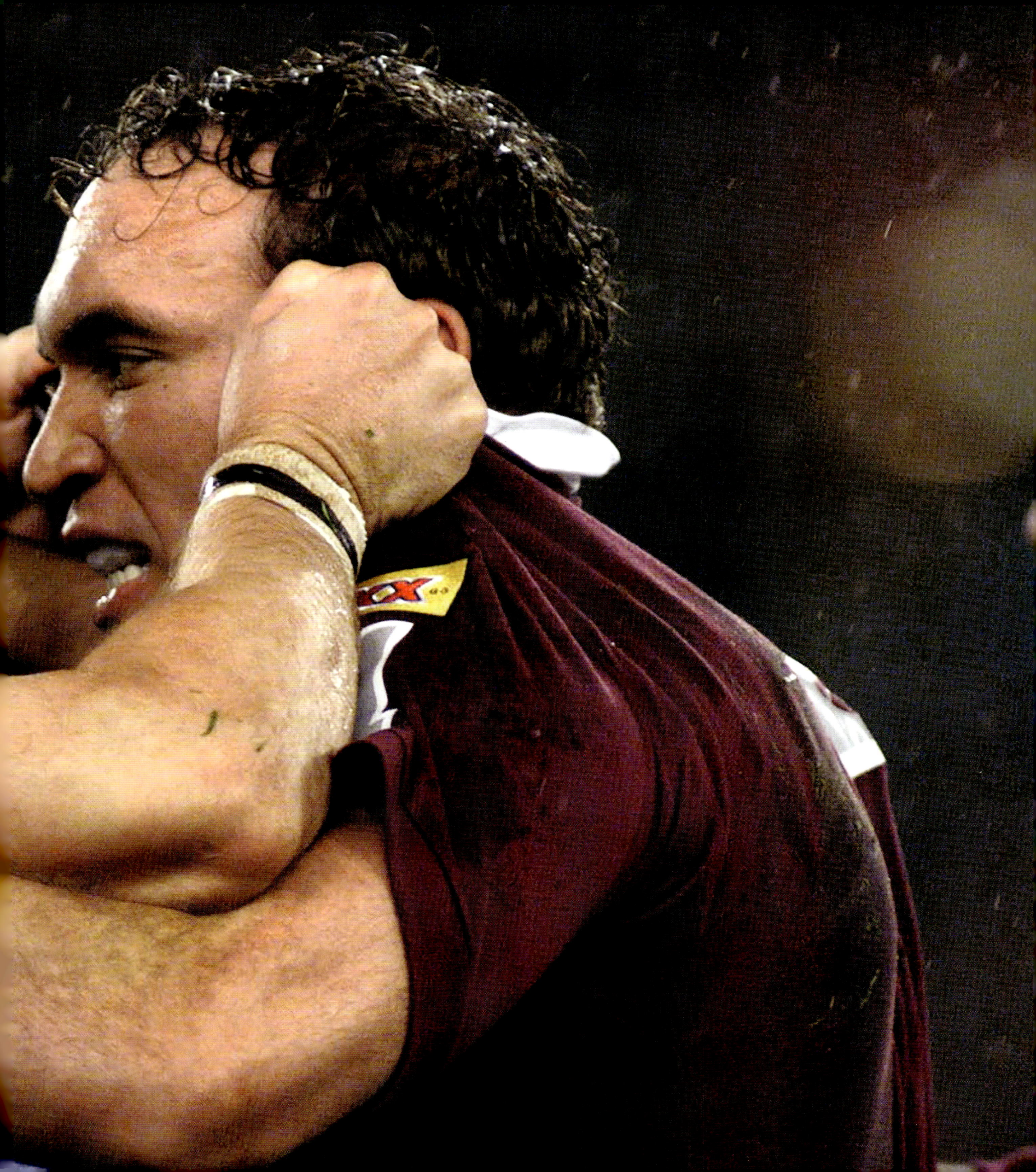

110 YEARS OF RUGBY LEAGUE | STATE OF ORIGIN

Men of influence: Origin founder Ron McAuliffe (left) and his successor Ross Livermore, who would spend 30 years at the helm of the QRL.

Heavy hitters: Former NSWRL chairman Kevin Humphreys strides to the middle of the Sydney Cricket Ground with Prime Minister Gough Whitlam.

Cop this: Artie Beetson was prepared to do whatever it took to get the Maroons home at Lang Park in 1980.

GO NSW
nib nib nib nib nib
TRY!
MAROONS
STATE OF ORIGIN
BROTHERS IN ARMS
XXXX

What started in 1999 with a couple of mates heading to Stadium Australia to cheer on NSW has grown into the fan phenomenon known as Blatchy's Blues, named after founder Dan Blatch. By 2015, the sea of blue had swelled to 15,000.

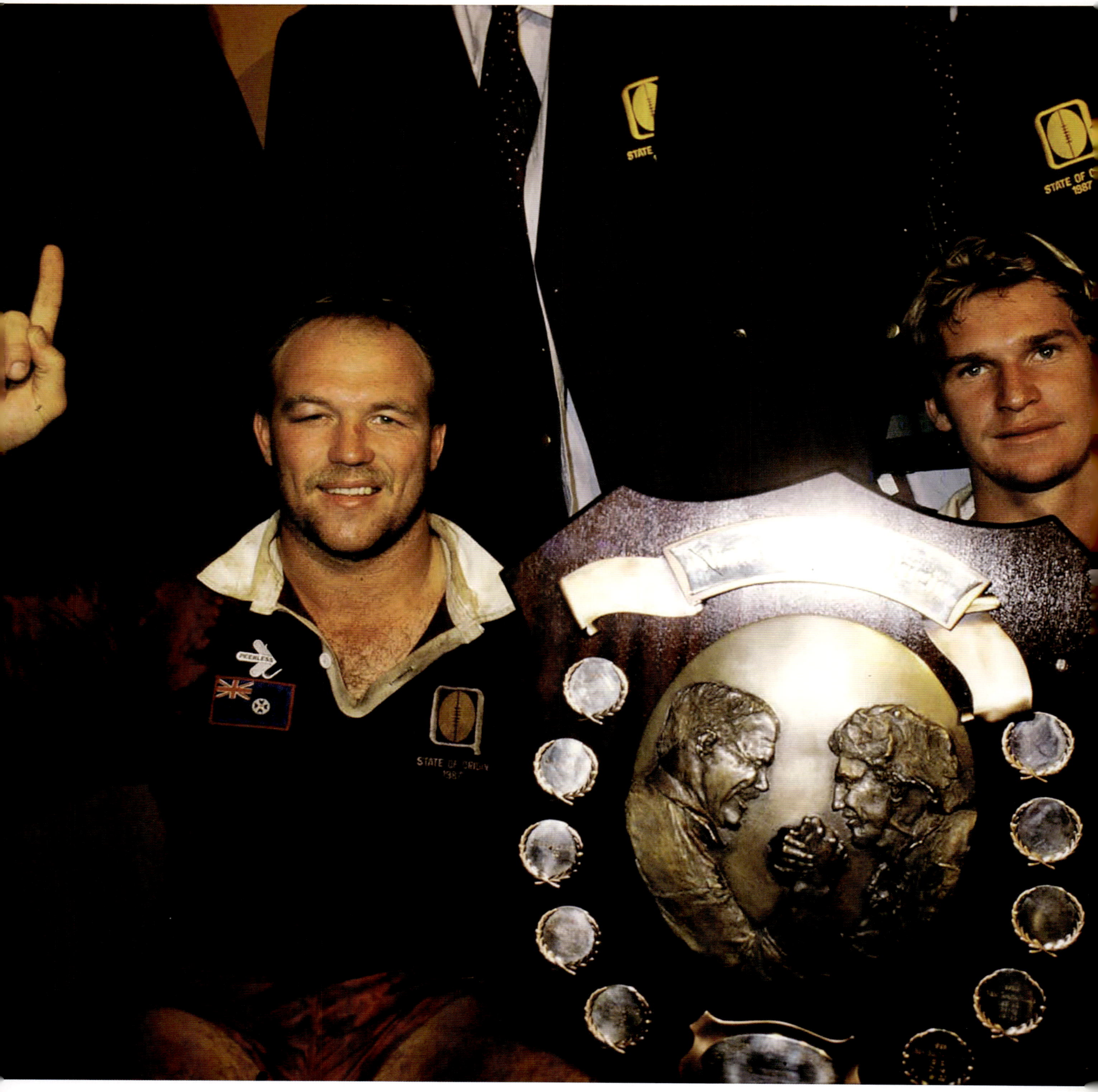
STATE OF ORIGIN
1987

110 YEARS OF RUGBY LEAGUE | **STATE OF ORIGIN**

Maroon to the bone: (Left) Wally Lewis and Allan Langer, the leader and the larrikin, played 65 Origins between them. (Above) When Chris Close was finished terrorising NSW on the paddock he slipped into a role as team manager and was the perfect man to inspire the likes of Gary Larson and Andrew Gee.

155

Origin powderkeg: NSW captain Ben Elias summed up this moment perfectly when he said, "If looks could kill, MG and Wally would both been six-feet under". It's Game Two, 1991 and Maroons captain Wally Lewis has had a gutful of Mark Geyer's strongarm tactics, so he decides to let the Blues enforcer know exactly what he thinks of him. Geyer would later quip that he wasn't sure whether to whack Lewis or ask for his autograph. Almost three decades later, it remains one of Origin's most talked-about showdowns.

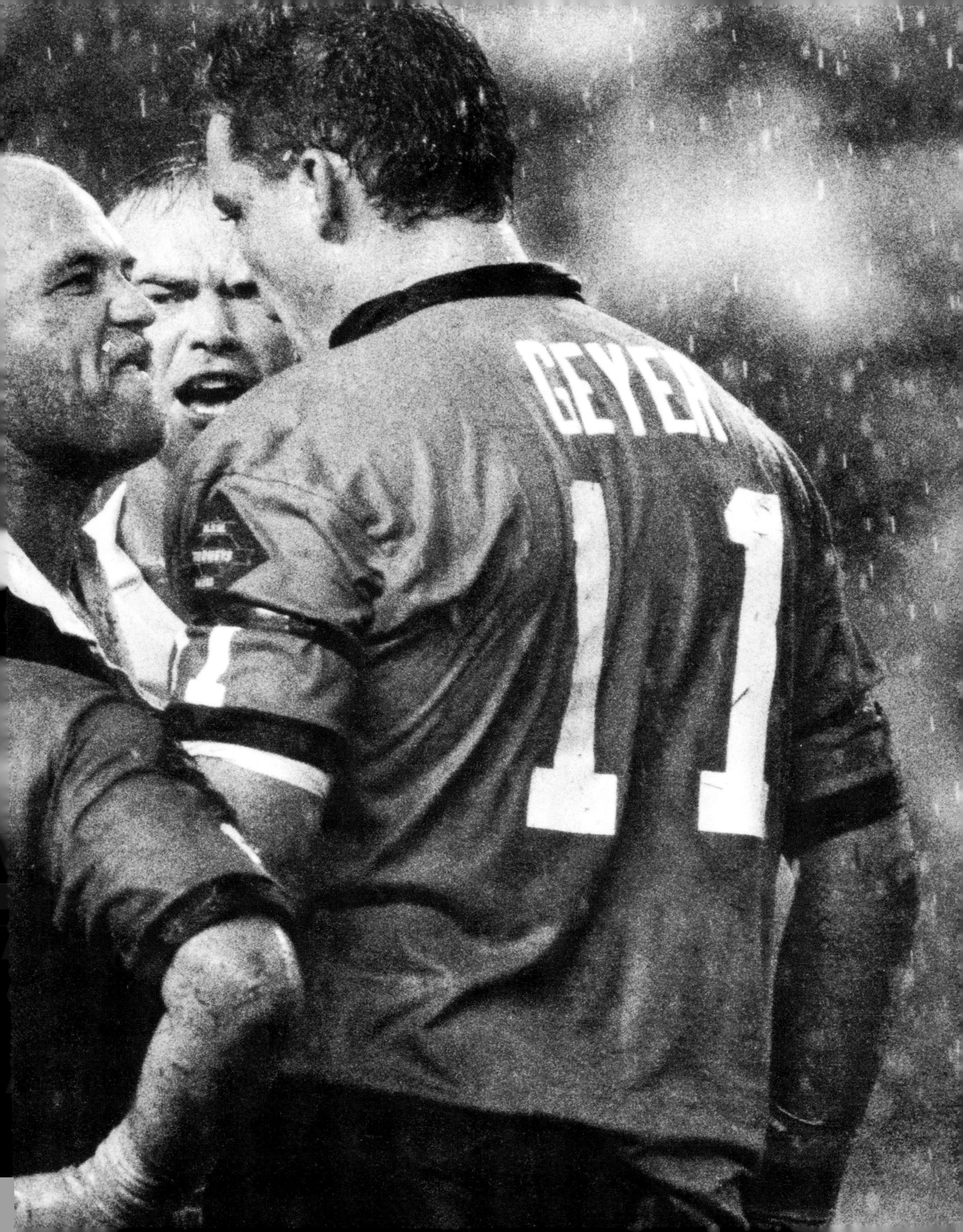
GEYER
11

Trevor Gillmeister epitomises everything the Maroons stand for and his nickname 'The Axe' fitted the man to a tee.

110 YEARS OF RUGBY LEAGUE | **STATE OF ORIGIN**

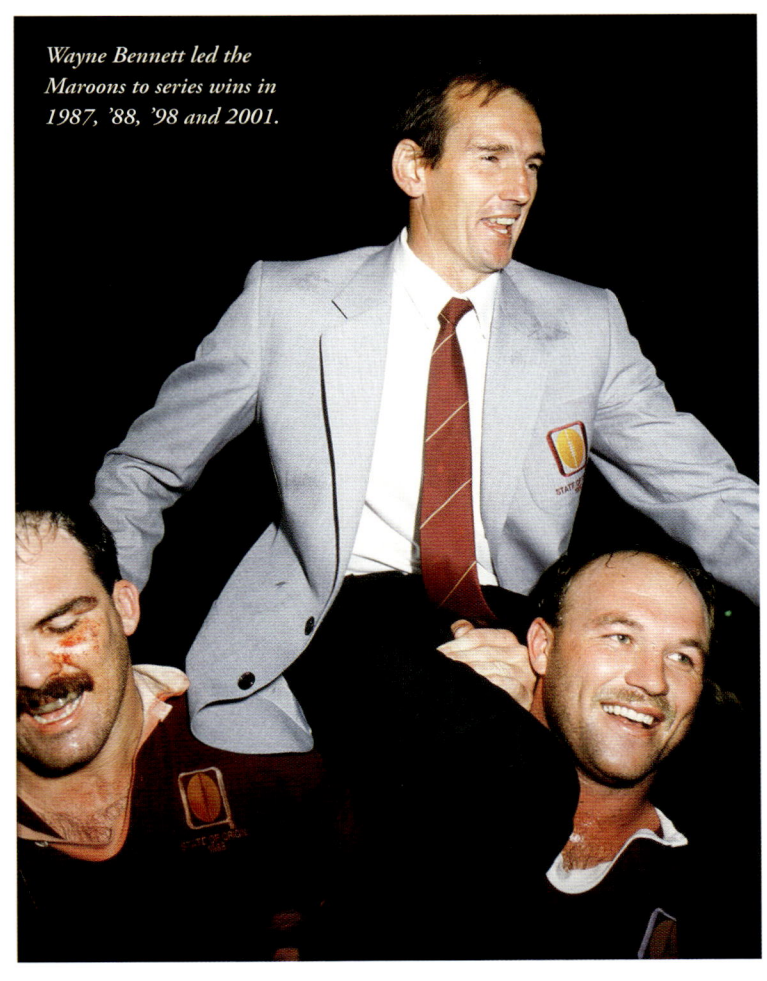

Wayne Bennett led the Maroons to series wins in 1987, '88, '98 and 2001.

Chris Johns grabbed a little piece of Origin history in Game One, 1989 when he became the first Queensland-based player in the NSW team. Johns was playing for the Broncos at the time and later revealed that club teammate Gavin Allen "amost killed me" on debut. No favours in Origin, even from the blokes you call mates every other day of the week.

159

Ben Elias spilt more than his fair share of blood for the Blues over the years, most famously in the series opener of 1992 in Sydney.

110 YEARS OF RUGBY LEAGUE | **STATE OF ORIGIN**

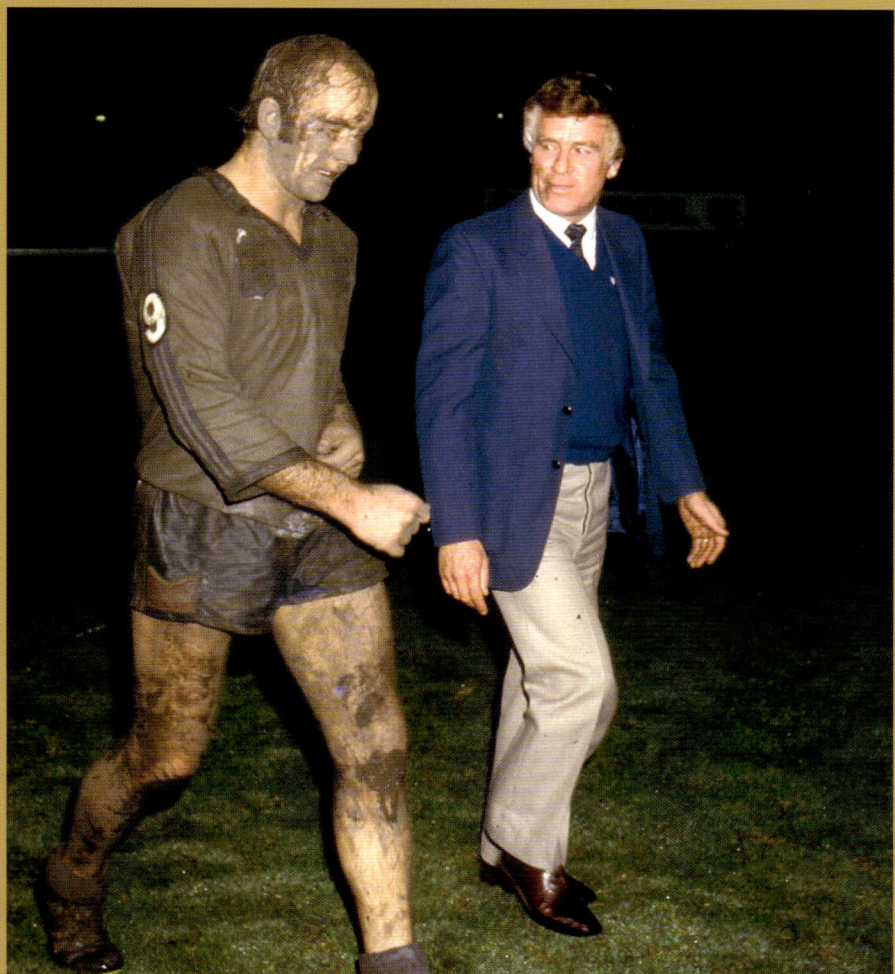

Mud and guts
(Above) Queensland prop Greg Dowling talks sideline eye Tony Megahey through the famous try he scored on an SCG mudheap in Game Two, 1984. The big man followed through a Wally Lewis chip kick which hit the crossbar and dropped straight down into in a puddle of water. Dowling showed superb skill to bend down and pick up the ball and slide over in the slush.

(Left) The Cootamundra kid, Paul Field, played two games for the Blues in 1983, under the astute guidance of coach Ted Glossop.

161

110 YEARS OF RUGBY LEAGUE | STATE OF ORIGIN

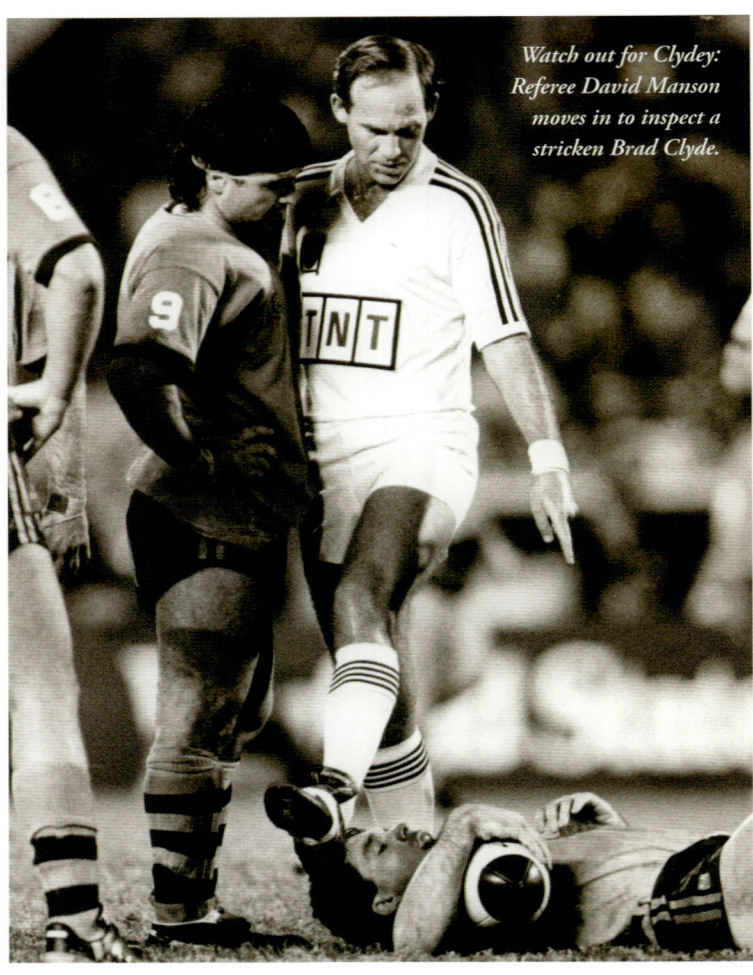

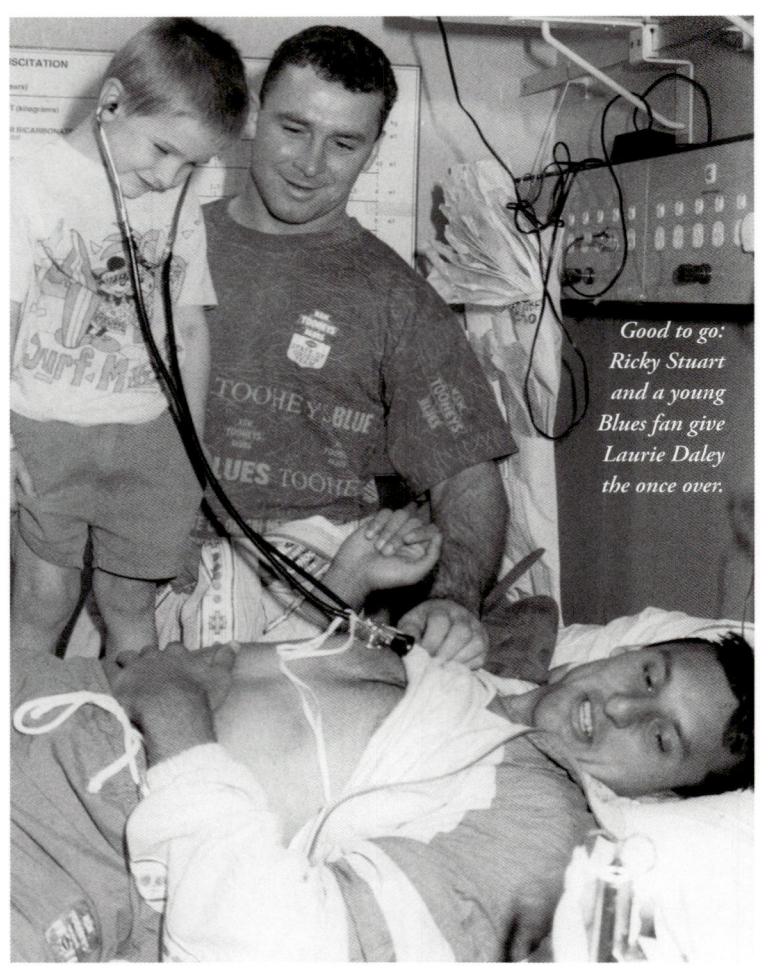

Watch out for Clydey: Referee David Manson moves in to inspect a stricken Brad Clyde.

Good to go: Ricky Stuart and a young Blues fan give Laurie Daley the once over.

Captain, my captain: Blues legend Laurie Daley led his men to three series wins on the trot from 1992-94. Just 22 when he took the reins, Daley recalls, "I was plucked from obscurity in terms of leadership. I wasn't captain of my club and I didn't know if I'd be ready but I knew I just had to go out there and be myself. I wasn't a big talker at that age so the best way to get those blokes to support me was to show I was prepared to do whatever it took for the team to be successful".

Leaders don't come any better than Cameron Smith, who assumed the Queensland captaincy full-time from Darren Lockyer in 2012 and seamlessly carried on the legacy established by men like Beetson, Lewis and Meninga. "Cam is a true leader in the sense that people want to follow him," Lockyer said in an interview last year.

XXXX
STATE OF ORIGIN
QLD
MAROONS
canterbury
Game 2
21 June 2017

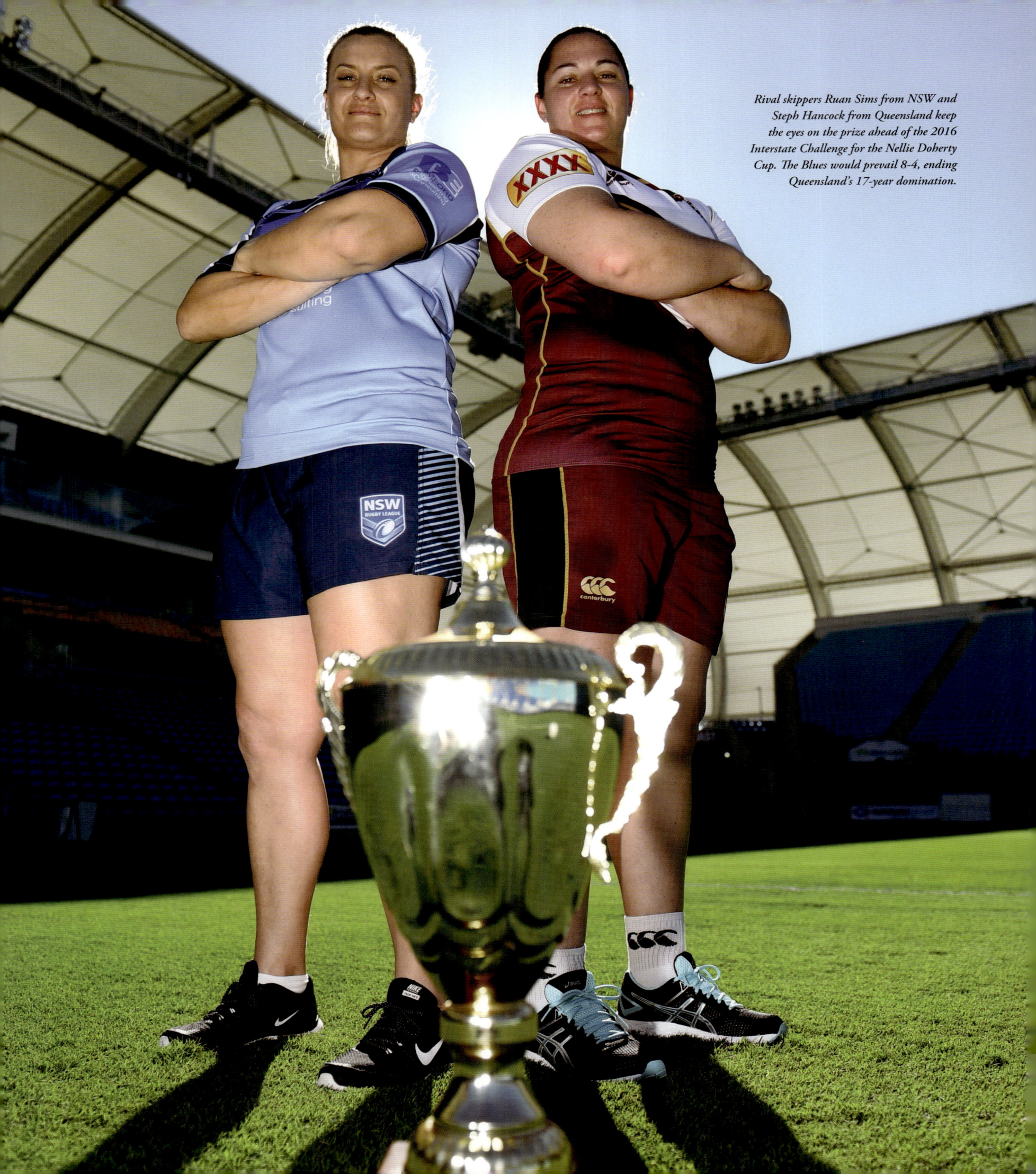

Rival skippers Ruan Sims from NSW and Steph Hancock from Queensland keep the eyes on the prize ahead of the 2016 Interstate Challenge for the Nellie Doherty Cup. The Blues would prevail 8-4, ending Queensland's 17-year domination.

110 YEARS OF RUGBY LEAGUE | **STATE OF ORIGIN**

Mutual respect: Blues forward Bruce McGuire and Queensland counterpart Bob Lindner after giving their all in another absorbing Origin contest — Game Two, 1989, won 16-12 by Lindner's Maroons.

THE FANS

Take away the dedicated diehards and you'd be left with a barren sporting landscape devoid of emotion – and no one wants that.

110 YEARS OF RUGBY LEAGUE | THE FANS

The passion of rugby league's true believers knows no boundaries. At home or away, by day or by night, come rain or shine, devoted fans turn out to cheer their team and hail their heroes. It's a ritual as old as the game itself. From the curious 3000 who turned out to watch the first ever premiership matches on April 20, 1908, at Sydney's Birchgrove Oval, to the world record crowd of 107,999 for the epic 1999 Grand Final between Melbourne and the Dragons at Stadium Australia, fans have been part of the game's fabric for 110 years.

When the stands are heaving and the emotion sweeps you away, there is no better place to be than at the footy, bonding with fellow fans and baying for opposition blood. Think raucous Redfern in the early '70s with McCarthy and Sattler in their premiership-winning pomp. Think of the Newcastle faithful in full voice at Marathon Stadium in '97, as Chief Harragon and Joey Johns ran amok. And think quaint Leichhardt Oval in Sydney's inner west, with the Tigers roaring and Laurie Nichols shadow boxing so hard he'd have put Jeff Fenech to shame. For Steve Roach, who gave his heart and soul in 185 games for Balmain between 1982-92, the memories of singlet-wearing superfan Nichols are as vivid and provocative as ever.

"Laurie was the greatest supporter in 110 years of footy – no-one even rivals him," Roach beams. "No matter whether you played Under-23s or Reserves or First Grade, Laurie was the first bloke you saw as you walked down the stairs to run onto Leichhardt Oval. He made you feel that good that his energy bounced off into you. He was a mascot without the suit.

"Everyone in the league loved Laurie. He'd be chanting and boxing and carrying on but no-one thought 'this bloke's an idiot'. He could walk in anywhere without a lanyard or a pass and that was an endearing trait to other clubs as well, and they knew he was rugby league through and through.

"Maybe today we are a bit precious about who can come in the sheds and who can't. We've lost that art of everyone belonging."

That sense of belonging, of sharing a common purpose, has rarely been better illustrated than the emotional scenes after the drought-breaking premierships savoured by Souths in 2014, North Queensland in 2015 and Cronulla in 2016.

The famous cardinal and myrtle already had 20 titles to their name, but it had been 43 years between drinks and patience was wearing thin. The Bunnies faithful had also been dealt the savage blow of being kicked out of the competition at the end of 1999, and spent two years in the wilderness as legal battles raged and fans of all clubs vented their anger at the expulsion. Thanks in no small part to the tireless efforts of club great George Piggins, the foundation club was reinstated in 2002 and set about the chase for that 21st premiership, which would eventually come on October 5, 2014.

For the Cowboys and Sharks, there was no silverware to show for years of toil. Two decades of Townsville torture. A half-century of heartache in the Sutherland Shire.

And while Souths fans could exhale with 15 minutes to play and savour a comfortable win over the Bulldogs in 2014, the Cowboys and Sharks armies were made to sweat and swear right to the sweet end. And in the Cowboys' case, into golden point before Johnathan Thurston's drop goal turned ANZ Stadium into a field of dreams realised.

To get an understanding of just how momentous that 17-16 win over arch-rivals Brisbane was to those fans who'd been along for the ride since the Cowboys' inception in 1995, look no further than Wayne 'Mad Dog' Evans.

The 51-year-old's 2000km drive to Sin City with wife Leonie in 2015 paid the ultimate reward – and he has the tattoo to prove it. Within weeks of the win, Evans was parting with $800 and putting up with seven hours of pain to have the names of all 17 players and coach Paul Green inked on his back, along with the Cowboys logo and an image of the premiership trophy as a permanent reminder of the night that changed his life.

"It had been my ambition from day one in 1995 to win a premiership and have that tattoo, and the boys did it for me," says Evans. "We jumped in the car on the Friday morning and got to Sydney on the Saturday. We had nowhere to stay but we found a little hole in the wall in the back blocks of Parramatta. I reckon it was the janitor's closet and they just banged a room number on it for Grand Final weekend!

"We had lived in the Broncos' shadow for a lot of years and we put up with being called easybeats, but no more. Hopefully I'll get a few more tattoos before I fall off the perch but nothing will be as special as the first one – that was 20 years in the making."

It's hard to imagine anything coming between Mad Dog and his team but sadly for Laurie Nichols, his love affair with the Tigers ended when they merged with Western Suburbs at the end of 1999.

For 30 years, Laurie had been to every home match, shadow boxing his way into the hearts of players and fans alike, but the merger meant that only a handful of games would be played at his beloved Leichhardt each season – a cruel blow to a man who had become as synonymous with Balmain as Roach, Pearce and hour-long waits for the toilet on the hill.

Just weeks before the merged entity was due to play its first match in 2000, Laurie passed away at the age of 77.

In June, 2015, when Leichhardt Council renamed the laneway outside the ground 'Laurie's Lane', councillor Darcy Byrne spoke for all league lovers when he said, "Laurie Nichols' legacy reminds us that rugby league belongs to the fans who follow it, not the people who profit from it".

Amen to that.

Balnain boys do cry: Steve Roach bids an emotional goodbye to the Leichhardt faithful and his good mate Laurie Nichols in 1992.

The mob has spoken: Cowboys fans let it all hang out at ANZ Stadium on Grand Final night 2015.

110 YEARS OF RUGBY LEAGUE | **THE FANS**

True colours: Wayne Evans rubber stamped his nomination for the title of league's most passionate fan when he celebrated the 2015 premiership with this work of art.

173

Hats off to Parra! When the crochet craze hit western society in the late '60s it filtered through to rugby league and also crossed over with the beer culture of the time and many people made their own hats incorporating the outside of cans. This beauty was made by a family member for Peter Cheeseman, who grew up in Granville and was an Eels fan, but lived for all his married life on the northern beaches in the heart of Manly territory. The fact it survived the fierce battles of the 1970s and '80s speaks for the quality of the craftsmanship. When the NRL Museum opened in 2012, Peter's daughter Vanessa was involved with the design and construction process and she kindly donated this item.

110 YEARS OF RUGBY LEAGUE | **THE FANS**

Flannel shirts, Parra flags flying and the SCG scoreboard ticking over with Parra points. Yep, it's the '80s alright.

175

110 YEARS OF RUGBY LEAGUE | THE FANS

Brisbane fans have had plenty to celebrate since the club's inception in 1988 and they have more members than any other club – but none were more dedicated to the cause than Brian Hall (above), who went to every home game between September 7, 2001 and May 24, 2013. To mark Brian's 250th consecutive game, the club struck a special commemorative jumper in his honour and it was presented to him by Justin Hodges. Brian passed away in 2016 but his contribution will never be forgotten.

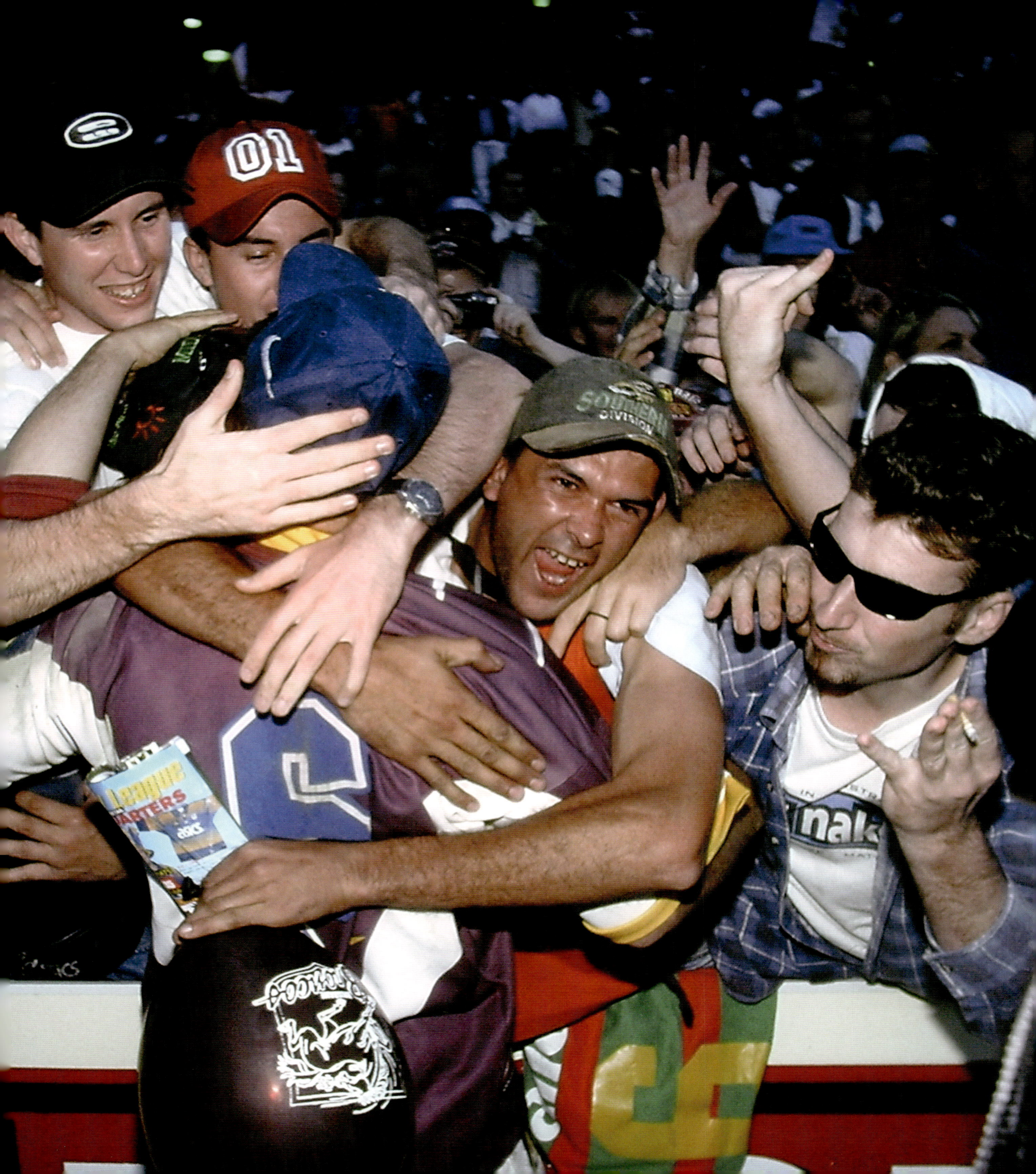
01
DIVISION

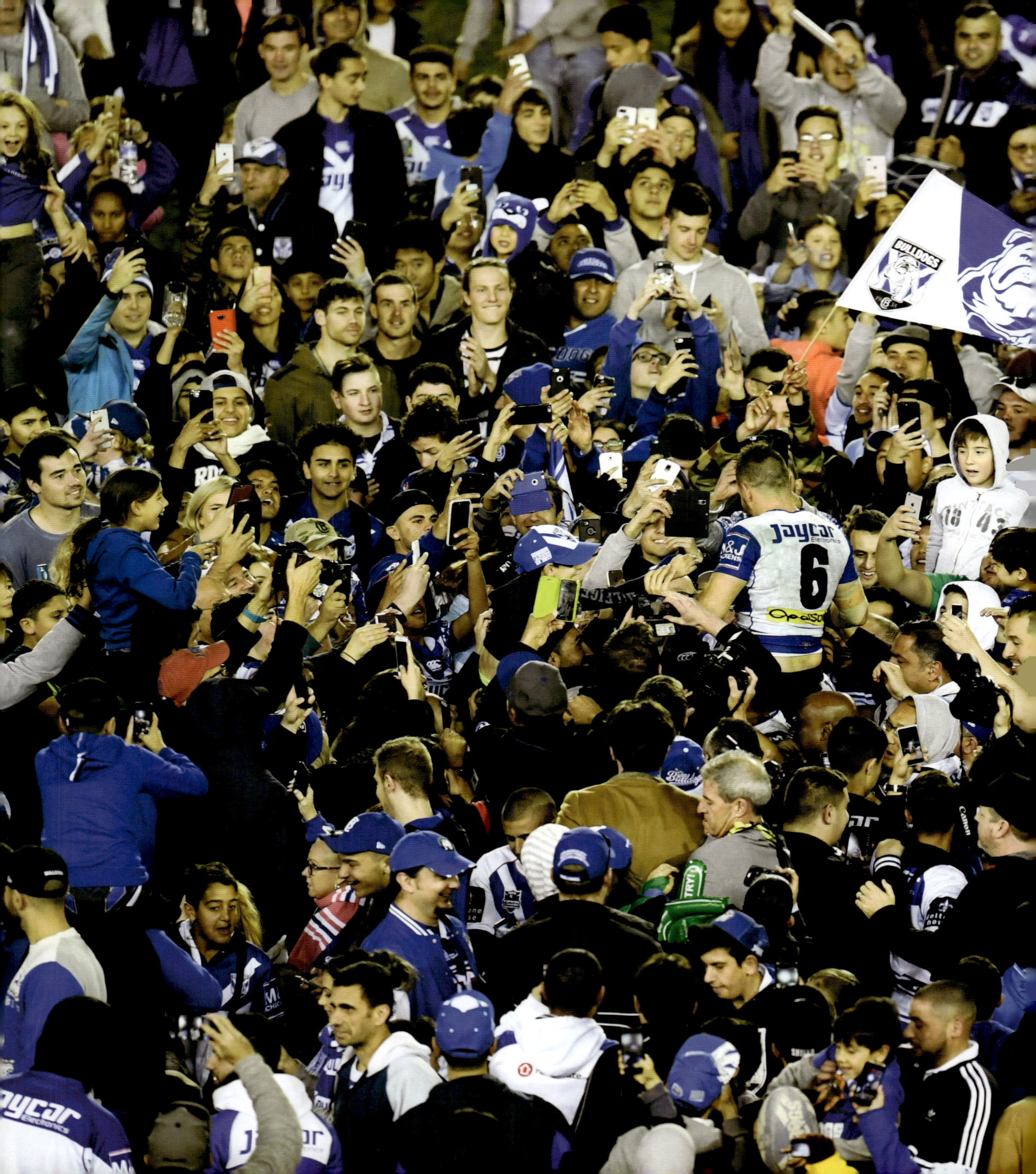

Where's Joshy? In emotional scenes at Belmore in round 18, 2017, beloved Bulldog Josh Reynolds played his final game at the club's spiritual home. The script couldn't have been written any better as the Dogs produced a miracle win after trailing Newcastle 18-8 with four minutes to play. "This will go down as one of my favourite days as a Bulldog", he told the faithful.

Bears fans vented their anger in 1997 as the Super League War split the game in two and threatened its very existence. North Sydney remained loyal to the establishment but were gutted two years later when forced into a merger with bitter rivals Manly.

The decison to cut foundation club South Sydney from the competition at the end of 1999 had the blood of league diehards boiling. The following year, more than 80,000 marched on Sydney's Town Hall demanding the Bunnies be reinstated.

110 YEARS OF RUGBY LEAGUE | **THE FANS**

Reggie The Rabbit readies himself to charge onto Redfern Oval and rev up the Rabbitoh faithful.

181

Year of the Knight: You couldn't have fitted one more fan into the centre of Newcastle as celebrations went into overdrive after the club's maiden title in 1997.

110 YEARS OF RUGBY LEAGUE | **THE FANS**

Newtown supporters have always been a special breed, and none moreso than June and Claude Hansell, who wore matching tracksuits in the days before supporters' merchandise. What really made this couple special, though, was the fact that Claude was blind and his wife acted as his eyes at games. They were fixtures at Henson Park for many years and at Newtown's last home game there in 1983 they were given a standing ovation by the crowd on the hill when they walked out at the end of the match.

110 YEARS OF RUGBY LEAGUE | THE FANS

It takes all sorts: the famous fig tree at North Sydney Oval (top) provided a sensational view but going to the bathroom or food stall was a mission. This Knights fan hurled himself into a bit of zorbing (above) while Raiders fans found their voices in a big way in 1989 as the Big Mal and co made Seiffert Oval a fortress.

184

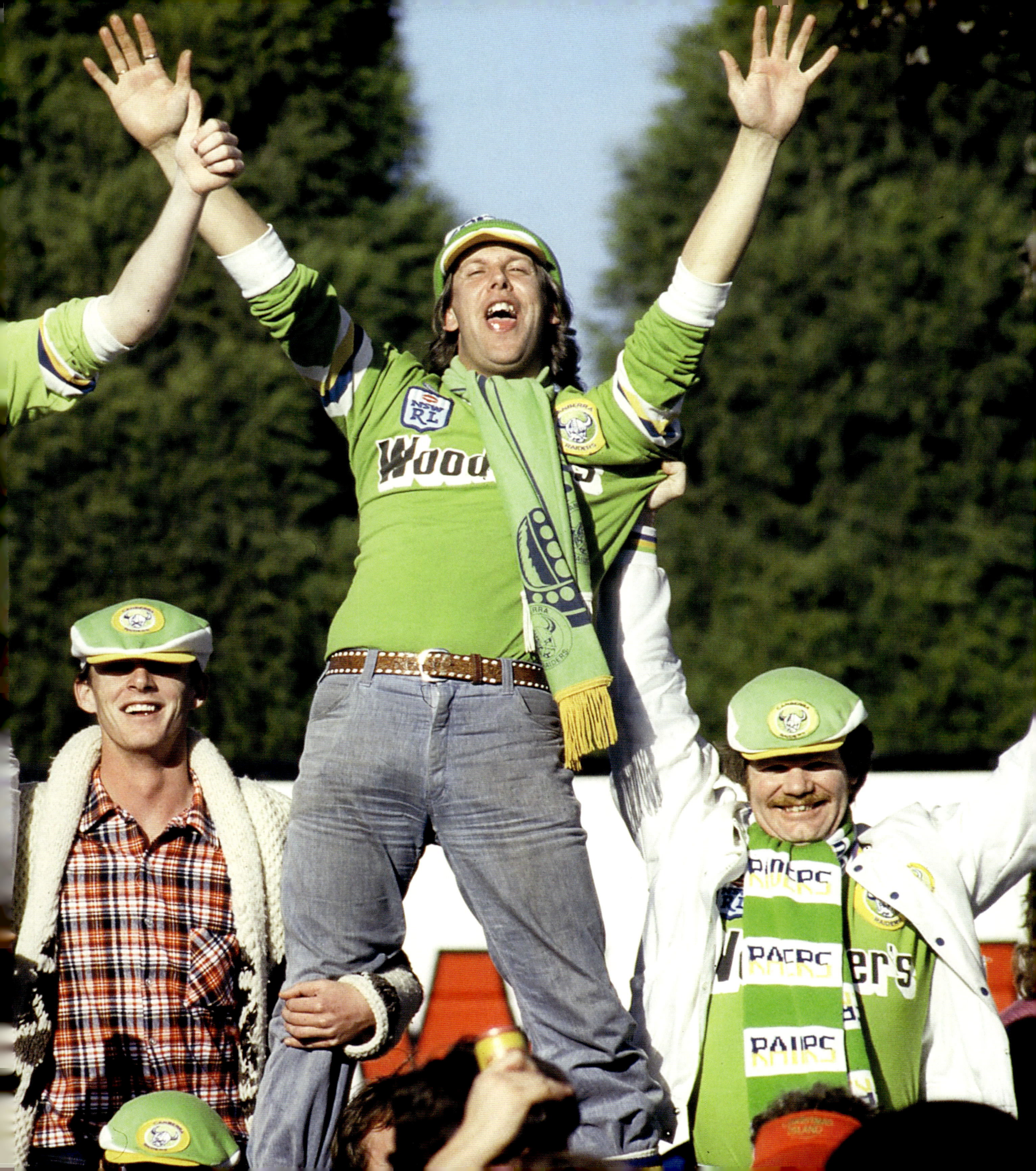
NSW
RL

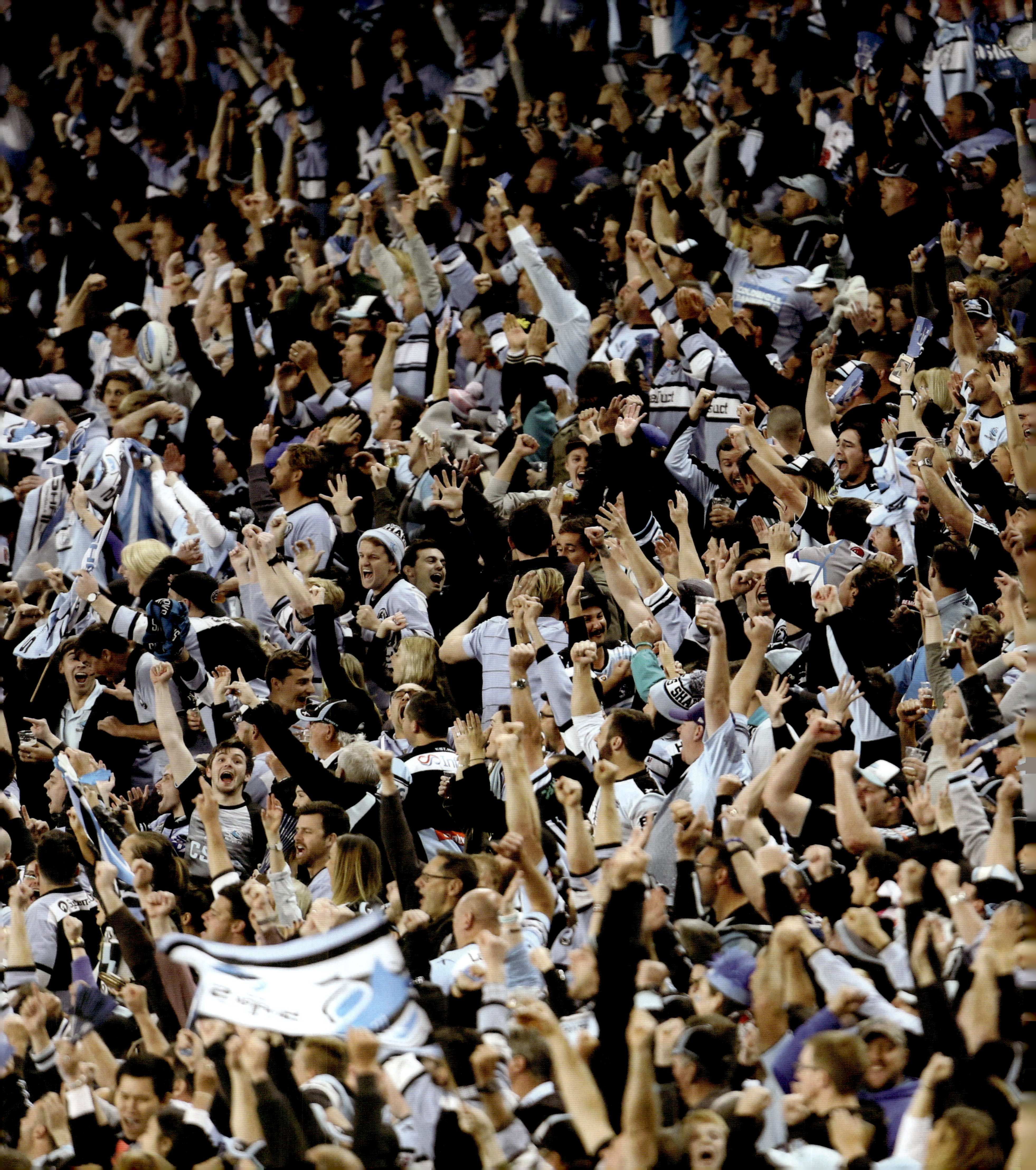

110 YEARS OF RUGBY LEAGUE | **THE FANS**

Legendary coach Jack Gibson had joked that "waiting for Cronulla to win a premiership is like leaving the porch lamp on for Harold Holt". Well, in 2016, the 50-year drought was broken, the Sharkies faithful finally had their moment and skipper Paul Gallen told them, "you can turn your porch lights off because we are coming home with the trophy".

187

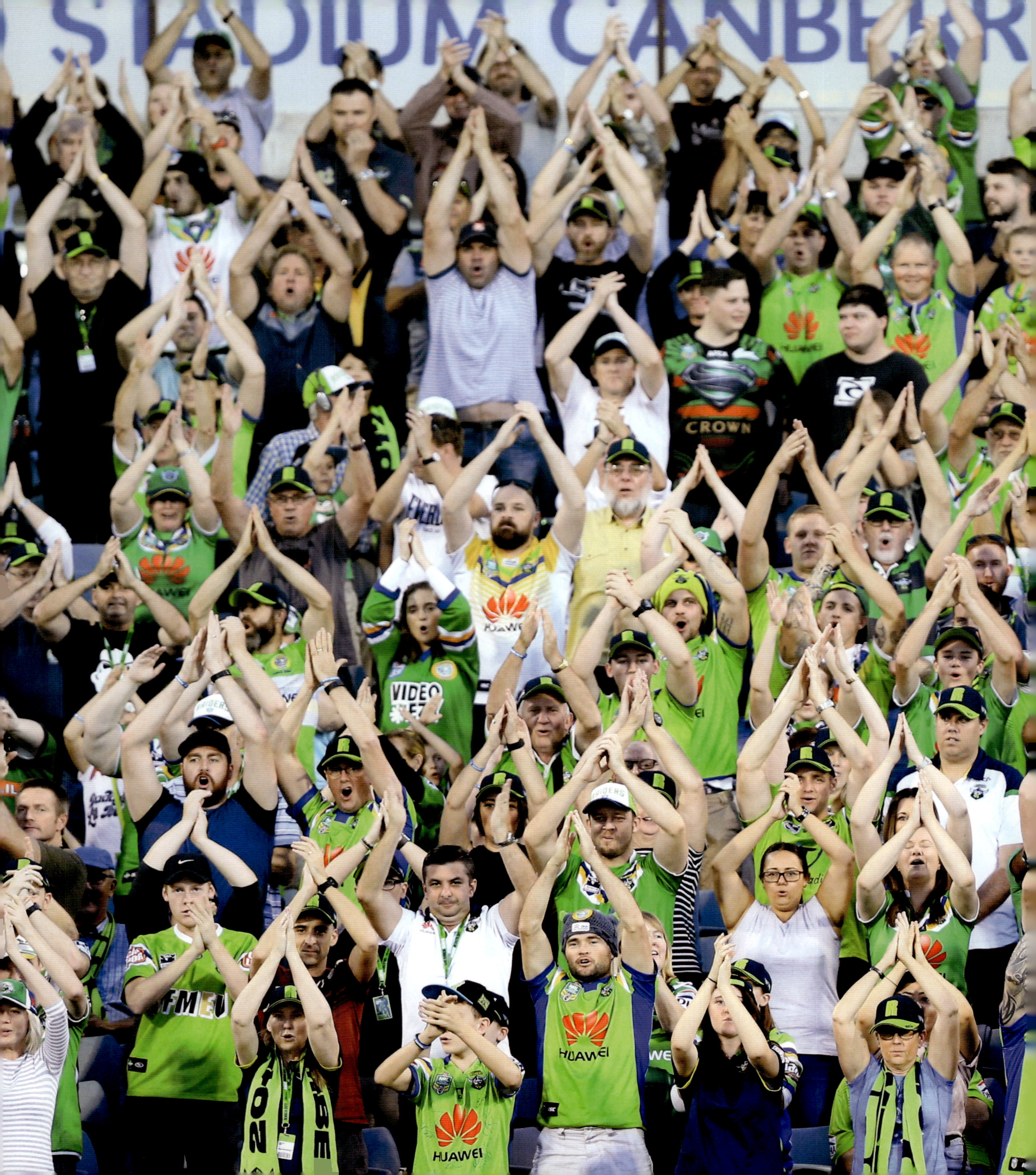
STADIUM
CROWN
HUAWEI

The Viking Clap rocks Raiders' home games and gives the Green Machine a massive lift as they hit the field.

Wayne 'Junior' Pearce was a hero to Balmain fans of all ages, giving his heart and soul to the Tigers through 192 games.

A handy trifecta: Wayne Pearce, Wally Lewis and Ben Elias are mobbed by fans at Leichhardt Oval in 1989.

Laurie Nichols' trademark shearer's singlet was his uniform of choice regardless of how cold it got at Leichhardt Oval in winter.

Michael Ennis was one of the heroes of Cronulla's emotional 2016 Grand Final win and the NRL's lead photographer Grant Trouville was on hand well after midnight at Southern Cross Group Stadium as delirious Sharks fans hailed the hooker.

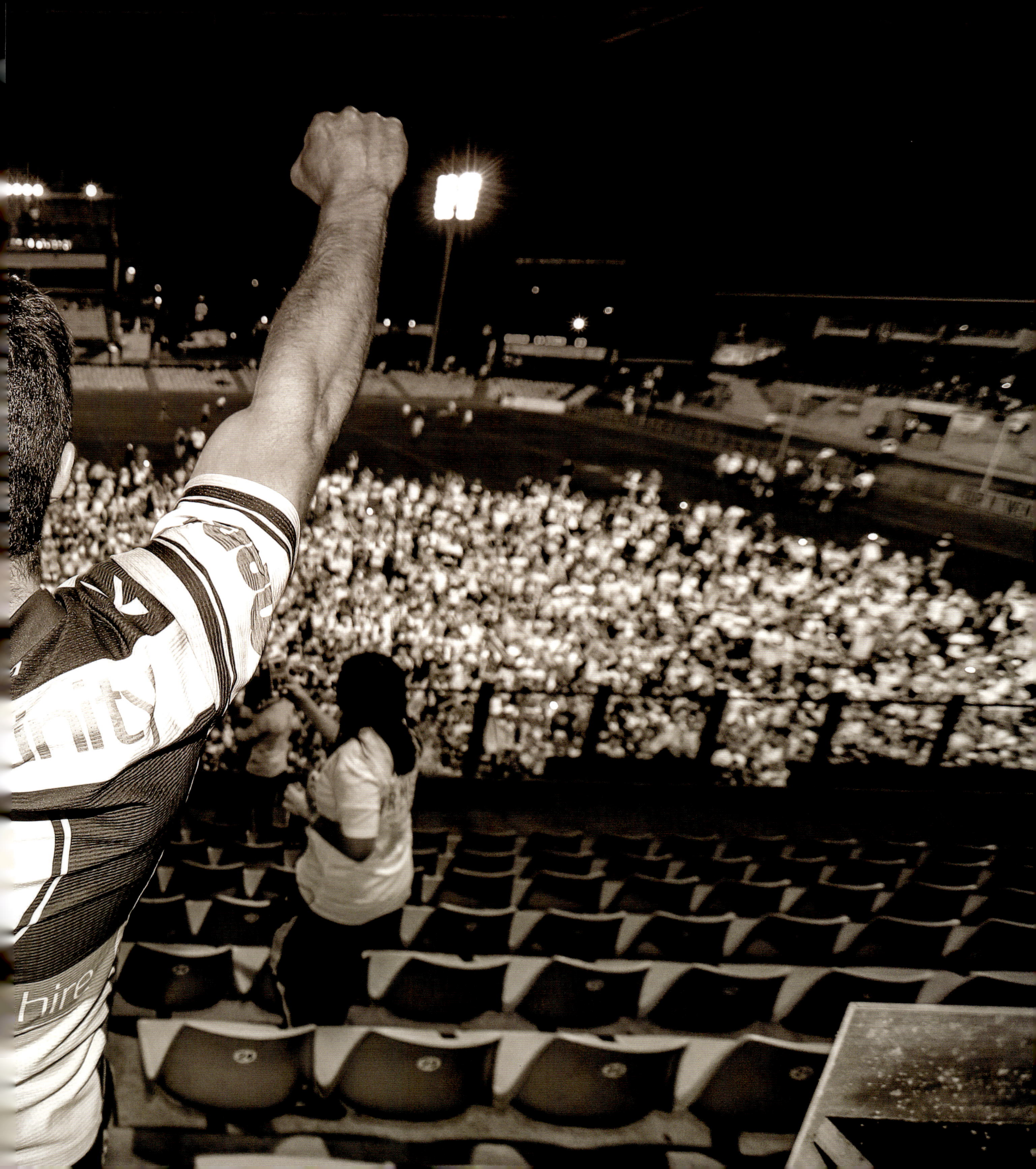

Whether at their spiritual home at Kogarah or on the road, the Red V faithful are among the NRL's most vocal and dedicated fans.

110 YEARS OF RUGBY LEAGUE | **THE FANS**

Painting the town maroon: Brisbane's iconic Caxton Hotel comes alive on Origin night as the locals bay for Blue blood.

195

THE RECORDS

Only the uniquely gifted and fabulously freakish can command a place in the record books of the greatest game of all.

110 YEARS OF RUGBY LEAGUE | THE RECORDS

When it comes to getting better with age, it's hard to imagine anyone coming close to 1960s iron man Billy Wilson and modern day marvel Cameron Smith.

Father Time sure as hell never caught up with the man they called 'Captain Blood' and he seems to have no idea where Captain Cam lives either.

Smith has already played more first-grade games than anyone in history and he's not done yet. Equal parts resilience and brilliance, the Melbourne maestro was 34 years and 265 days old when the Storm kicked off their 2018 premiership campaign against the Warriors. His longevity is more remarkable given the added physical and mental toll of playing Origin and Test footy for more than a decade.

"His mental toughness is remarkable. No one can break him," says fellow Maroons legend Johnathan Thurston.

"To play in the position he has for as long as he has and play that amount of games, you need to be quick between the ears and mentally tough and he has both those qualities in spades.

"I played a lot of footy with Darren Lockyer and I used to think he was four or five sets ahead of everyone else on the field, but Cam is eight or nine sets ahead.

"Cam is so calm and controlled, you wouldn't know if you're 10 points behind or 10 in front. That's what I've tried to take away from playing alongside him. I play with my heart on my sleeve and I'm easy to read but he's got the best poker face of all.

"He's already played more games than anyone in history and the legacy he leaves in all three teams (Storm, Queensland and Australia) is unparalleled. For a bloke from Logan from the south side of Brisbane to go on and captain his state and his country and achieve what he has, it's an amazing story."

Smith may be setting records to last a lifetime but there's one mark he'll be quite happy not to reach – Wilson's milestone as the oldest first-grader at 40 years and five days when he ran out for Norths against Canterbury in 1967.

Two decades after starting his career with St George, the man dubbed Captain Blood because he was split open so many times, was still going strong for the Bears. "Billy was from the Noel Kelly and Frank Farrell school of retaliate first, ask questions later," jokes NRL historian Terry Williams.

Legendary tales of Billy's bravery abound, like the day he broke his arm in the first half of a game against Balmain in 1965 but went back onto the field and defied intense pain to set up the winning try.

And if you want to talk about hard men for a hard road, look no further than the unfashionable, underrated, unbreakable Luke Douglas.

The former Shark and Titan holds the record for most consecutive first grade games – a staggering 215 on the trot from 2006-14. Through 146 games for the Sharks and 69 for Gold Coast, the prop from Yamba on the NSW north coast dug deep to keep getting on the field even when the odds were against him – like midway through 2011 when knee and ankle injuries seemed certain to end the streak at 133 games.

"We were playing Melbourne on a Sunday and about 20 minutes into the game I took a hit-up and got bent back and I was sure I had done my knee," Douglas recalls. "The early diagnosis was a medial ligament and gone for six weeks. I was in the big brace straight away and I was pretty down.

"I thought I'd be out the next week but I worked my butt off in rehab and then Mum came to the rescue with an ice compression machine she bought off the internet.

"I had an ankle problem as well as the knee and I had the ice buckets in the lounge room non-stop and after a couple of days I told the physio I was feeling more confident. He said if I could get through the captain's run the day before the next game he'd give me the green light.

"It was a short turnaround from the Storm game to our next game against the Broncos on the Friday but I got there. I was heavily strapped for the next month but I pushed through."

Pushed through the pain. Turned his head away when painkilling needles were administered. And carved out a record streak that was ended late in the 2014 season not by injury but by an ASADA suspension dating back to the Sharks' 2011 supplements program.

It's a cruel twist of fate that still burns Douglas, who is adamant he did nothing wrong and didn't want to sign anything that admitted guilt. The deal that had been struck meant Douglas would miss just three NRL games but it was enough to snuff out his unbroken run.

"I was pretty gutted because it was taken out of my hands but I'm pretty proud of that record looking back on it," he says. "My goal when I came into the NRL was just to play one game on TV so to play 215 games in a row is pretty cool."

Another of the game's revered tough nuts was Sid "Sandy" Pearce, the champion Easts hooker who was still going strong in his late 30s. In 1921, Pearce played the last of his 14 Tests for Australia at the ripe old age of 38 years and 158 days. Renowned for his superhuman strength, Pearce made the Kangaroo tour in 1908 and missed out in 1911-12 before returning in 1921. Legend has it he was fond of a stink on the field – but only after his team-mates had stoked the fire.

"He was pretty quiet but if he got hit, he'd see red, so sometimes the hit would come from his own second-rower who'd reach through and give him one to get him angry. Sid would pop his head up and say, 'right it's on, let's go'," recounts Terry Williams.

As Cameron Smith has proved hundreds of times over, it's the mild mannered ones you need to watch the closest.

Fitting tribute: Johnathan Thurston and Cameron Smith were honoured with a testimonial match at Suncorp Stadium in February, 2018.

Iron men: Jason Taylor played 194 successive games between 1992-2000 before Luke Douglas (right) eclipsed that mark in 2014. The durable Douglas is typically modest when reflecting on his record: 'I never reached too many top speeds so I wasn't going to pop too many hamstrings like the power guys'.

110 YEARS OF RUGBY LEAGUE | **THE RECORDS**

Loyal clubman: Nathan Hindmarsh built a career on hard yakka and loyalty, racking up 330 games for Parramatta between 1998 and 2012. 'Hindy' is the only man to play 300 games for the Eels.

No.1 gun: Hailing from Woy Woy on the NSW central coast, Graham 'Wombat' Eadie has the distinction of scoring the first four-point try in the game's history, in 1983. The powerful fullback became the first Australian to win the Lance Todd Trophy for man of the match in the English Challenge Cup Final when he led Halifax to victory over St Helens in 1987.

RECORD NUMBERS

MOST POINTS IN ONE MATCH
45 Dave Brown, Easts v Canterbury
Sydney Sports Ground, May 18, 1935
5 tries, 15 goals

MOST POINTS IN ONE SEASON
Hazem El Masri
Bulldogs 2004 (342 pts)
16 tries, 139 goals

MOST TRIES IN FIRST-GRADE
212 Ken Irvine 1958-1973

MOST CONSECUTIVE GOALS
35 Hazem El Masri, Bulldogs, 2003

MOST PREMIERSHIPS AS A COACH
8 Arthur 'Pony' Holloway
7 Wayne Bennett
5 Jack Rayner
5 Ken Kearney
5 Jack Gibson

MOST POINTS ON DEBUT
22 (1 try, 9 goals)
Amos Roberts, Dragons v Warriors
WIN Stadium, May 6, 2000

MOST FIRST-GRADE TITLES
Souths **21**
St George **15**
Easts (Sydney Roosters) **13**

YOUNGEST FIRST-GRADE PLAYERS
Ray Stehr **16** years and **85** days
Easts v Norths, April 25, 1929
Jack Arnold **16** years and **220** days
Wests v Balmain, April 25, 1936

OLDEST FIRST-GRADE PLAYERS
Billy Wilson **40** years and **5** days
Norths v Canterbury, June 4, 1967
Tedda Courtney, **39** years and **311** days
Wests v Balmain, July 5, 1924.

El Magic: Prolific Bulldog Hazem El Masri was given an emotional send-off by the Blue and White Army after his final game against the Warriors in round 25, 2009.

110 YEARS OF RUGBY LEAGUE | **THE RECORDS**

The indestructible Billy Wilson was dubbed 'Captain Blood' by footy writer George Crawford and wore the title as a badge of honour.

203

110 YEARS OF RUGBY LEAGUE | THE RECORDS

Boy wonder: Nathan Cleary topped the NRL pointscoring charts in 2017 with 216 points, the first 19-year-old since South Sydney's Harold Horder in 1913 to finish the season as leading scorer.

Mike Cleary had the distinction of representing his country in three sports – rugby league, rugby union and as a sprinter at the 1962 Commonwealth Games in Perth.

Ray Stehr was just 16 years and 85 days old when he took the field for Eastern Suburbs against Norths on April 25, 1929 – the youngest first-grade player in history. Stehr's story is more remarkable given he was diagnosed as a cripple when he was eight and was unable to walk for two years after a blood clot had gathered at the base of his spine.

110 YEARS OF RUGBY LEAGUE | THE RECORDS

A world record crowd of 107,999 packed into Stadium Australia for the 1999 Grand Final between the Melbourne Storm and newly formed joint venture club St George Illawarra Dragons. The Storm would prevail in a classic showdown but not before excitement machine Nathan Blacklock (left) scored one of the great Grand Final tries, gathering a kick on the fly and running 70 metres to bring the pro-Dragons crowd to its feet. And when it comes to heaving Grand Final crowds, the grand old Sydney Cricket Ground (right) provided an atmosphere that had to be felt to be believed.

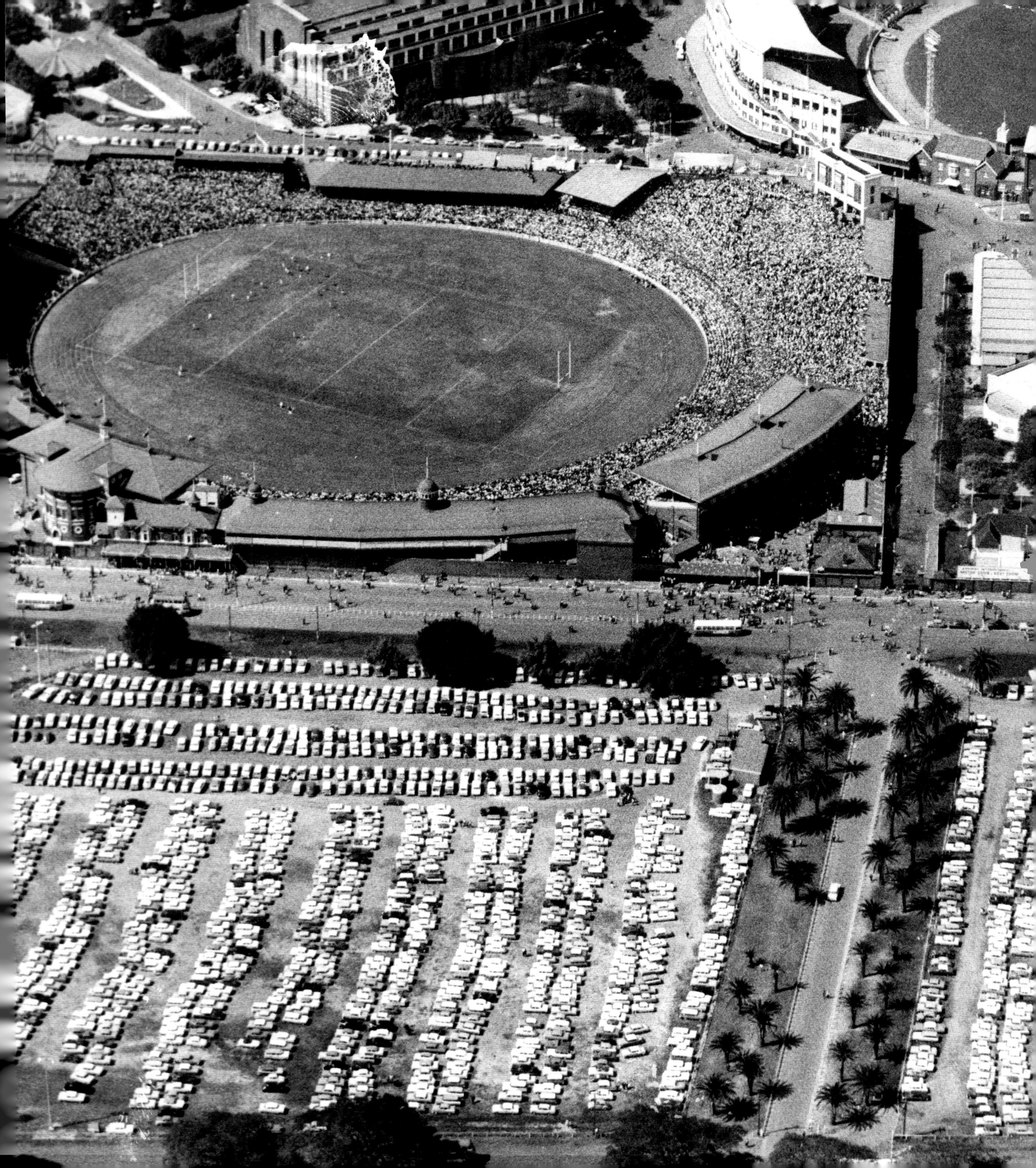

One-club legend Andrew Ettingshausen peeled off 328 games for the Sharks between 1983 and 2000 before turning his love for fishing into a post-footy career in television.

110 YEARS OF RUGBY LEAGUE | **THE RECORDS**

Patrons at the Gerringong Hotel on the NSW south coast have long enjoyed sharing an ale and a tale with Parramatta legend Mick Cronin, whose tally of 865 career goals is the sixth highest in the game's history. His tally of 1971 points is seventh all-time behind Hazem El Masri, Cameron Smith, Andrew Johns, Jason Taylor, Johnathan Thurston and Daryl Halligan.

Champion Rooster Kevin 'Horrie' Hastings collected the Rothmans Medal as the game's best and fairest player in 1981. The irrepressible halfback played 228 games for the foundation club.

110 YEARS OF RUGBY LEAGUE | **THE RECORDS**

Dual in the crown: Arthur Summons played 10 rugby Tests for the Wallabies in the late '50s before switching codes and winning nine caps for the Kangaroos.

Six of the best: Kangaroos flyer Valentine Holmes scorched Fiji for an Australian record six tries in the 2017 World Cup semi-final at Suncorp Stadium in Brisbane.

Peter Sterling was the supreme playmaker for Parramatta as they collected four premierships during the 1980s. In 1986, Sterling was the inaugural winner of the Clive Churchill Medal, awarded to the man of the match in the Grand Final.

110 YEARS OF RUGBY LEAGUE | **THE RECORDS**

A magical moment for Andrew Johns in 2001, receiving the Clive Churchill Medal from Churchill's widow Joyce.

Sharks stalwart Luke Lewis took home the Clive Churchill Medal in 2016 after a typically wholehearted performance.

213

110 YEARS OF RUGBY LEAGUE | THE RECORDS

Famous Amos: At just 19, Dragons speedster Amos Roberts set an NRL record for most points on debut when he piled on 22 points against the Warriors in 2000.

The Great Survivor: Wayne Bennett reached a remarkable milestone in 2018 when he coached his 800th premiership match. It all began at Canberra in 1987 when he was appointed co-coach of the Raiders and since then the wily 68-year-old has led Brisbane to six premierships and St George Illawarra to one. Testament to King Wayne's longevity is the fact that second place on the list of all-time games coached is Tim Sheens with 669.

Terry Lamb began his 350-game career at Western Suburbs (above) in the early '80s, winning the Dally M Medal in 1983, before joining the Bulldogs in 1984. By the end of the decade, 'Baa' had become the first man to score 100 tries and 1000 points for the same club.

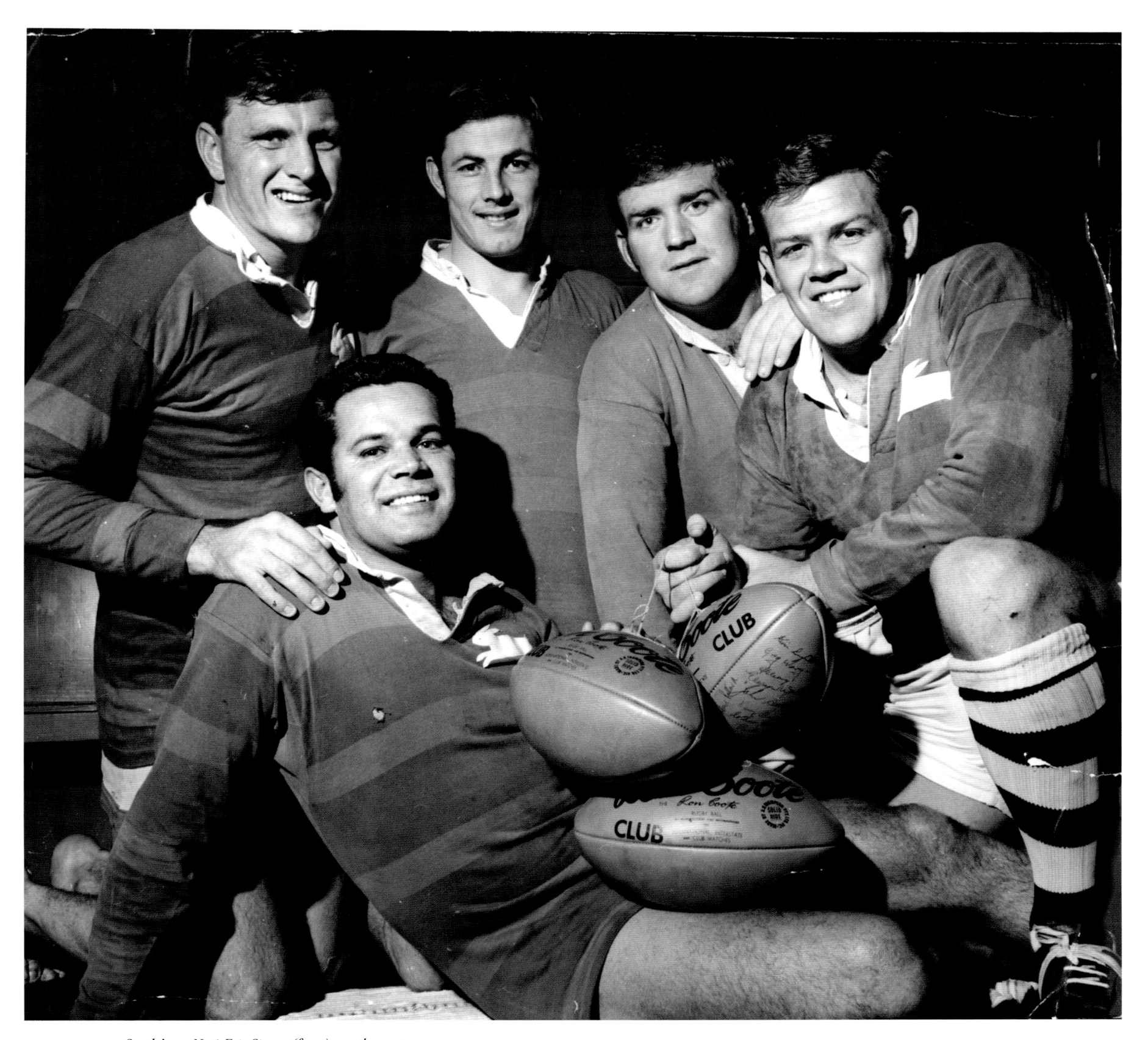

Souths' gun No.1 Eric Simms (front) was the master of the field goal when the one-pointer was in vogue. Simms holds the record for most field goals in a match (5 v Penrih in July, 1969), most field goals in a season (29 in 1968) and most field goals in a career (86).

110 YEARS OF RUGBY LEAGUE | **THE RECORDS**

The Bradman of league: Easts centre Dave Brown's record of 45 points in a single match will never be touched and his mark of 38 tries in a season in 1935 seems certain to be his forever as well.

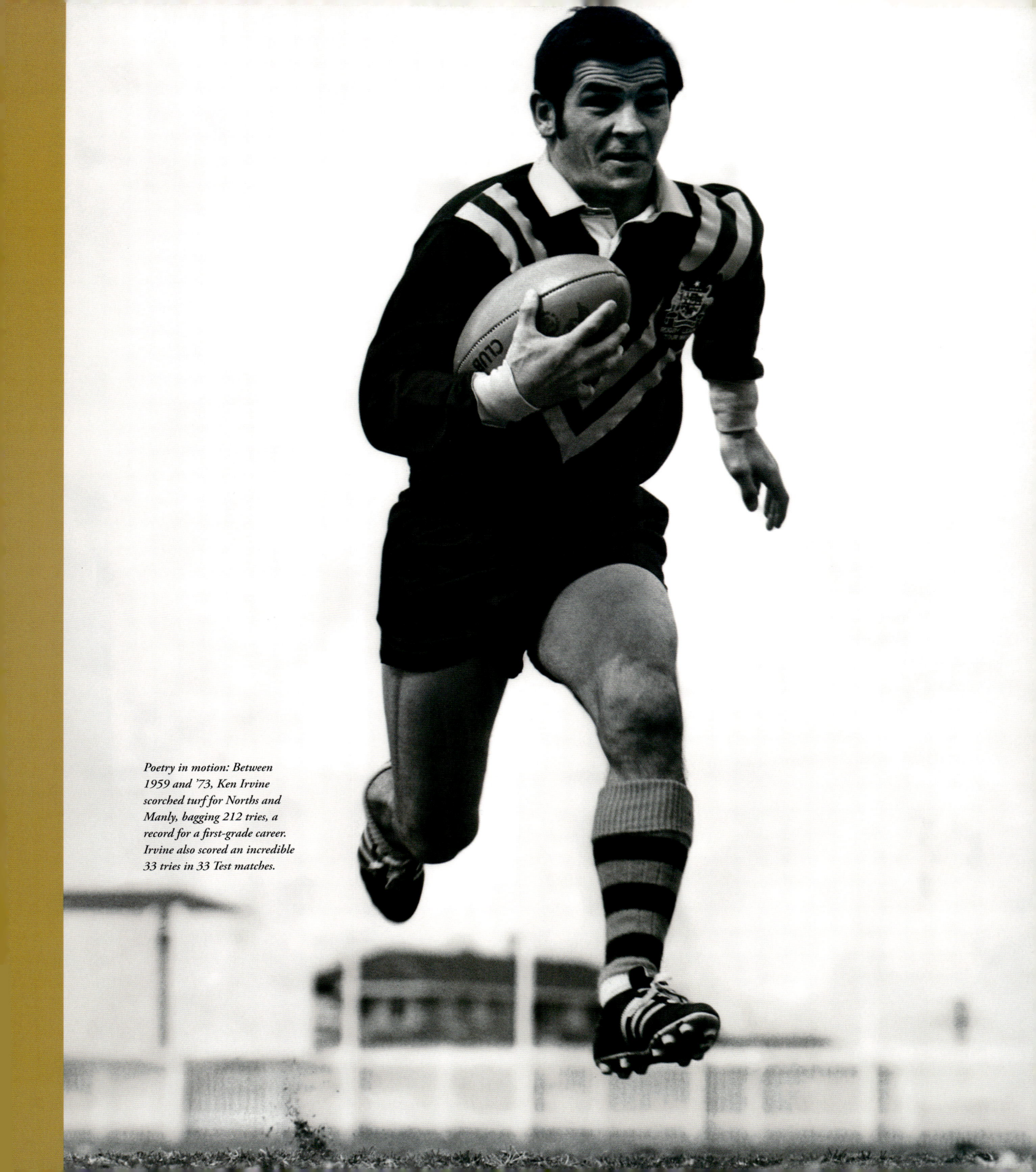

Poetry in motion: Between 1959 and '73, Ken Irvine scorched turf for Norths and Manly, bagging 212 tries, a record for a first-grade career. Irvine also scored an incredible 33 tries in 33 Test matches.

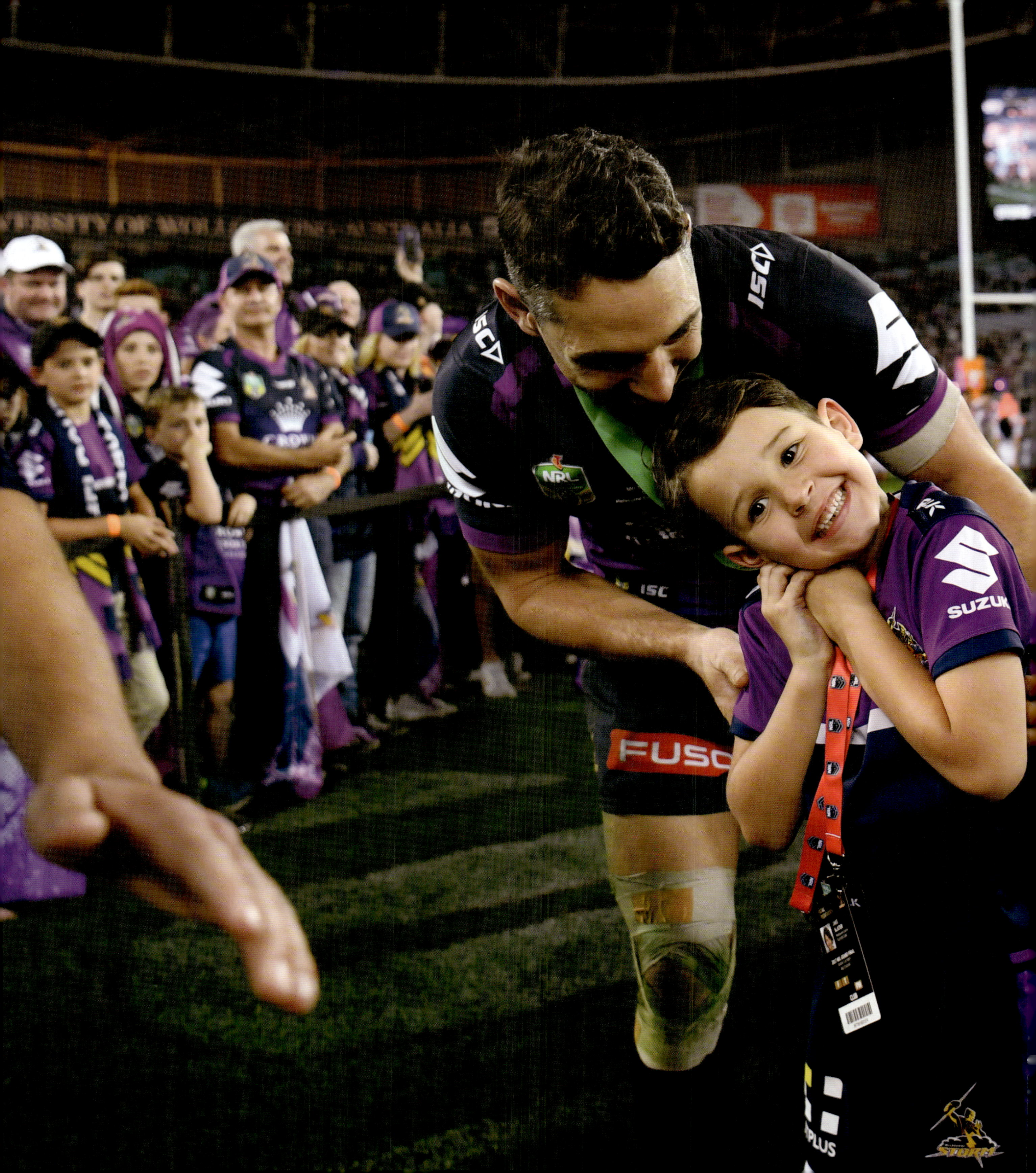
ISC
NRL
SUZUK
FUSC

110 YEARS OF RUGBY LEAGUE | **THE RECORDS**

Billy and the kids: Melbourne maestro Billy Slater won his second Clive Churchill Medal in 2017 as the Storm downed the North Queensland Cowboys. Slater became just the second player to win two Churchill Medals, after Canberra's Bradley Clyde in 1989 and '91. Slater's son Jake was suitably impressed by Dad's achievement.

221

Cowboys maestro Johnathan Thurston joined the 300 Club in round one, 2018, and will call time on a magnificent career at the end of the season.

INDEX

A
Annandale 68

B
Balmain 68, 170
Arthur Beetson 15, 38, 144
Alf Blair 68
Dave Brown 15, 38
Frank Burge 18

C
Clive Churchill 15, 38
Chris Close 38, 144
Brad Clyde 68
Arthur Conlin 68
Ron Coote 15, 38
Cumberland 68

D
Laurie Daley 15, 68, 144
Brett Dallas 144
Luke Douglas 198

E
Graham Eadie 15
Eastern Suburbs. 68
Steve Edge 68
Wayne Mad Dog Evans 170

F
Frank Farrell 198
Terry Fearnley 68
Brad Fittler 15, 144
'Jersey' Flegg 15
Bob Fulton 15, 38

G
Dane Gagai 38
Reg Gasnier 15, 38
Jack Gibson 68
Trevor Gillmeister 144
James Giltinan 18
Ryan Girdler 144
Glebe 68
Paul Green 170

H
Arthur Halloway 68
Paul Harragon 170
Arthur Hennessy 15, 68
Kevin Humphreys 144
Ben Hunt 15

I
Ben Ikin 144
Ken Irvine 15

J
Andrew Johns 15, 38, 170
Brian Johnston 144

K
Ken Kearney 68
Bill Kelly 68
Noel Kelly 38, 198
Brett Kenny 68, 144

L
Allan Langer 15, 38, 144
Graeme Langlands 15, 38
Edward Larkin 18
Glenn Lazarus 68
Wally Lewis 38, 112, 144
Bob Lindner 144
Darren Lockyer 112
Cliff Lyons 15

M
Manly 18
Mariners 68
Willie Mason 15
John Mayes 15
Mal Meninga 38, 68, 144
Dally Messenger 18, 68
Darcy Moore 170
Paddy Moran 18
Steve Morris 144
Chris Mortimer 144
Steve Mortimer 144
Ron McAuliffe 144
Bob McCarthy 170
Paddy McCue 18
Chris McKivat 18
Frank McMillan 68

N
Newcastle 68
Newtown 68
Laurie Nichols 170
North Sydney 68

O
John O'Neill 112
Bob O'Reilly 112

P
Sid Pearce 198
Wayne Pearce 15, 170
George Piggins 170
Norm Provan 38, 68

R
John Raper 38
Tommy Raudonikis 68
Jack Rayner 68
Steve Renouf 15
Steve Roach 15, 170
Geoff Robinson 15

S
John Sattler 15, 170
Eric Simms 170
Billy Slater 15
Billy Smith 15
Cameron Smith 198
Harry Sunderland 18
South Sydney 15, 68
St George 68
Ricky Stuart 68

T
Victor Trumper 18
Johnathan Thurston 15, 38, 170, 198

V
Paul Vautin 144

W
Ian Walsh 68
Steve Waugh 112
Western Suburbs 68
Sonny Bill Williams 15
Terry Williams 18, 68, 198
Billy Wilson 198
Peter Wynn 68, 144

By purchasing this Official Licensed Product you are supporting
the growth & development of Rugby League and your Club.
Proudly produced under licence by Bauer Media Pty Ltd.

® TM The NRL Logo and NRL Club Logos are registered trademarks
owned by the Australian Rugby League Commission or NRL Clubs.
The NRL Clubs are licensed to use these Logos.

Join **nrl.com** for free member benefits

Published in 2018 by Bauer Media Books, Australia.
Bauer Media Books is a division of Bauer Media Pty Ltd.

Bauer Media Books
Associate Publisher Sally Eagle
Creative director Hannah Blackmore
Author Martin Lenehan
Designer Bernhard Schmitz
Consultant Ewen Page
Picture Editor Bonnie-Maree Weigand
Sales Manager David Scotto (DScotto@bauer-media.com.au)

With thanks to
NRL Historian Terry Williams
NRL Lead Photographer Grant Trouville
NRL Photos & Film Matt Long

Photos NRL Imagery, NRL archives, Getty Images, Fairfax, Newspix, Alamy

Printed in China
by Leo Paper Products Ltd

A catalogue record for this book is available
from the National Library of Australia.
ISBN: 9781925694871 (hardback)

© Bauer Media Pty Limited 2018
ABN 18 053 273 546
This publication is copyright. No part of it may be reproduced or
transmitted in any form without the written permission of the publishers.

Published by Bauer Media Books,
a division of Bauer Media Pty Ltd,
54 Park St, Sydney; GPO Box 4088,
Sydney, NSW 2001, Australia
Ph +61 2 9282 8618; Fax +61 2 9126 3702
www.bauer-media.com.au

Order books
phone 136 116 (within Australia)
or order online at www.magshop.com.au